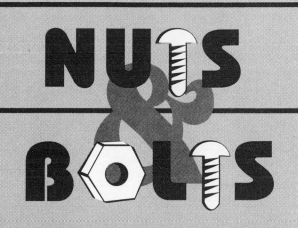

NUTS & BOLTS

ISSUES

FOR

Small Group Leaders

William J. McKay

Nuts & Bolts Issues for Small Group Leaders

1996 Revised and Expanded Edition
Copyright © 1996 by Stephen Ministries
First printing, August 1994
Copyright © 1994 by Stephen Ministries
All rights reserved

ISBN 0-9633831-6-7
Library of Congress Catalog Card Number 96-69489
Printed in the United States of America

Scripture quotations are from *The New Revised Standard Version Bible,* copyright © 1989 by the Division of Christian Education of the National Council of the Churches of Christ in the USA and used by permission.

Write to: Stephen Ministries
               8016 Dale
               St. Louis, MO 63117-1449

Cover design: Elizabeth Wright
Typesetting: Aleta Bird
Printing: Plus Communications

00 99 98 97 96
  5 4 3 2 1

*To Martha, Barb and Don, Harry and Martha,
Bill and Eileen, Rev. Chandler—and all the other
group leaders whose names I can't remember—
who taught me the joy of knowing and
serving Jesus in small groups.*

Contents

Acknowledgments

I want to acknowledge the help many people gave to the process of writing this book. Without their help and encouragement, there would have been no book. If I have left anyone out, I hope they will forgive my oversight.

Nuts & Bolts was written as part of the development of the ChristCare Series system of small group ministry. 250 Pioneer-Partner congregations tried out the ChristCare Series and contributed their experience, expertise, and insights about serving Jesus through small group ministry. I am especially grateful to those who shared their wisdom about practical small group leadership challenges and solutions, and thus contributed greatly to the usefulness of this book.

This book would never have existed without the help of my colleagues on Stephen Ministries' Pastoral and Executive Staff: Kenneth Haugk, Joan Haugk, David Paap, Gary Voss, Michael Welch, and Stephen Glynn. These colleagues read the manuscript and offered helpful suggestions. They were at the center of the team that created the ChristCare Series and its unique way of doing small group ministry, which I have tried to set out in this book. I am grateful for the privilege of working with such gifted and dedicated colleagues.

I have had the privilege of working with many other gifted, deeply committed colleagues at Stephen Ministries. While all played an important role in making this book possible, I want to recognize a few who were most closely involved in this project. Grace Hughey edited the book (as well as thousands of pages of other ChristCare Series materials) and asked questions that led to greater clarity. Antony Hebblethwaite shared his experience as a small group leader, student of theology, and a sensitive communicator, and in doing so made this book better. Peggy Kuethe managed typesetting for this book, as well as the entire ChristCare Series. Elizabeth Wright designed the entire book—covers and layout—with her usual eye for beauty and functionality. Marlene Muller contributed her publishing expertise to insure the professional quality of the product. Joel Keen and Elizabeth Cook provided invaluable support while this book was being written. Candace Czernicki wielded a razor-sharp editor's pen and taught me to write more clearly. Joel Bretscher's editing improved everything he touched. Sydney Donahoe's readable writing helped make this book more organized and understandable.

I also had the privilege of working with Kari Vo who helped write, edit, and organize the book's content. Kari played a major part in getting this project off the ground and determining its final shape.

I thank God for all these colleagues. I pray that the Holy Spirit will use our work to help create missional small groups that make a difference in this world as Jesus' servants.

Preface

What a joy it is to lead a small group. I have led small groups and also participated in groups led by others, and God has blessed each group with growth, care, and the joy of seeing fellow members become Jesus' more fully devoted followers. I wish I could share the experiences of every small group leader who reads this book. You have a wonderful adventure ahead of you.

I want to share a few thoughts about this book that will help you get the most out of it.

Christian Small Groups

This book focuses on *Christian* small groups. There are certainly many kinds of small groups that do not emphasize Christianity, and their group leaders may find some benefit in this book. This book, however, is as deliberately Christian as I am able to make it.

The ChristCare Series

Nuts & Bolts is one of the books people read as part of their training to serve as ChristCare Group Leaders—that is, small group leaders in congregations that are enrolled in the ChristCare Series. You can learn more about the ChristCare Series in the appendix at the end of this book.

You will notice occasional footnotes that describe elements in the Christ Care Series. Although these are primarily for the benefit of readers training to become ChristCare Group Leaders, they may also help other readers to better understand what the ChristCare

Series is like, and pick up some hints about how to make any small group more effective and enjoyable.

Helping Groups Serve

Nuts & Bolts describes many decisions small group leaders typically make. These decisions range from refreshments to meeting place and time, from child care to sharing leadership with other group members. Although many people don't realize it, these decisions are all *missional* decisions. They all affect how your group serves Jesus.

I've tried to emphasize the missional aspect of these decisions in order to help small groups overcome a temptation many of them face. Small groups can be such wonderful experiences that members are sometimes tempted to try to keep the experience to themselves. Accidentally or deliberately, they start to keep others out of the group and reserve all the group's time and energy just for the people already in it.

Groups run into two problems when they give in to this temptation. One is that they miss out on all the blessings that come from serving others. By this self-centered behavior, they may even ruin the group they are trying to preserve. The other problem is that these groups neglect Jesus' commands to serve as he served and to reach out and make disciples. Jesus said, "If any want to become my followers, let them deny themselves and take up their cross and follow me. For those who want to save their life will lose it, and those who lose their life for my sake will find it." (Matthew 16:24-25) Jesus invites small groups to give away the blessings they receive and trust him to continue to provide everything they need.

So, when your group makes any decision, make it a missional decision. Decide to meet in the place where you will best serve Jesus. Choose a group emphasis that will best serve Jesus. Each of the decisions discussed in this book offers you the same opportunity—to find ways to lead your group into

iv

more and more service. You'll find that the more you serve, the greater the blessings you'll experience.

How This Book Is Organized

This isn't the kind of book you have to read from beginning to end in order to use or understand it. It is more of a reference book, and is organized to help you find the information you need quickly. The chapters are very short and usually cover one particular subject. I hope that makes the book easy for you to use.

How This Book Refers to God

Some books never use pronouns to refer to God, but this book is not like that. Referring to God with pronouns makes him seem personal and real. Without pronouns, God can seem like some far off, abstract concept—not the loving Father Jesus shows us.

However, personal pronouns, in English, require a gender. When you use pronouns for God you run up against the truth that God is not really male or really female (and certainly not an *it*.) God goes far beyond our understanding of gender. Both women and men are made in God's image:

So God created humankind in his image, in the image of God he created them; male and female he created them. (Genesis 1:27)

Since we need to use pronouns to write about our loving, relational God, and since attributing gender to God is inaccurate, what do you do? Jesus is the one who shows us most clearly what God is like, so he is the one who makes the decision for us. Jesus always referred to God as his Father, and this book will follow his example.

Jesus Will Work in and through You

"Now you are the body of Christ and individual members of it" (1 Corinthians 12:27). Jesus will speak, forgive, bless, heal, and renew through you and the group members you serve—and you are going to have the time of your life in the process.

Keep your eyes on Jesus and see all the wonderful things he is going to do as you attend to the nuts and bolts of leading your small group. God bless, and have fun leading your group.

William J. McKay
Pentecost, 1996

PART ONE

Deciding What Your Small Group Will Do

Christian small groups exist to glorify and serve God, and to help members care for one another and grow as Jesus' disciples. To that end groups usually do four activities:

- community building and care;
- Biblical Equipping™[1];
- prayer and worship;
- missional service.

Part one focuses on these activities. You will learn how to lead your small group in all four activities, and how to emphasize some in order to fulfill your group's particular mission and meet members' needs.

---

[1]Biblical Equipping is the term that the ChristCare Series uses for small group Bible study. It is a special way for small group members to have a life-changing encounter with God's Word during and between group meetings. This book will use the term *Biblical Equipping* to refer to what is traditionally called small group Bible study. To learn more about this process, see *Biblical Equipping: God's Word in Your World* by David A. Paap (St. Louis: Stephen Ministries, 1996).

CHAPTER 1

Building Community in Your Small Group

One of the main reasons people are attracted to small groups is because they want an opportunity to get to know other Christians in a relaxed and personal setting. A small group is one of the few places left in the world—and even in many congregations—where people can know others, and be known, on a deeply personal level. Jesus' presence in Christian small groups adds an even deeper dimension to relationship building.

Community building is what happens as group members learn to know and trust one another, and become more comfortable sharing personal thoughts and feelings. Building community is especially important at the group's start, as members take their first tentative steps in trusting one another, and you as their leader. But even in mature groups, community building remains important. It helps members know and trust one another more and more deeply.

How to Build Community in Your Group

Trust and community don't just happen. You will need to plan community building opportunities for your group. You can help your group build community in many different ways and through many different activities. Here are a few suggestions about how.[1]

Encourage Members to Share Their Stories

One way to get to know others better is to learn

---

[1] *Beginnings: A ChristCare Group Experience,* is a small group course that helps groups build community during their first eight times together. The *Beginnings* course is part of the ChristCare Series.

about their personal histories. Plan group sharing times in which group members talk about their families, their childhood, their hobbies, and their jobs. You can also encourage this kind of self-disclosure by playing community-building games and selecting discussion topics that ask members to talk about themselves. As you lead your group in community building, be sensitive to the fact that personal sharing might be difficult for some group members. Always give group members the option to "pass" during such an activity.[2]

Encourage Members to Share Their Feelings

Encourage group members to share their feelings when they talk about their lives or about Scripture. As the members of a group learn to trust one another, they will feel more comfortable sharing their feelings. At first they may only share feelings that are socially acceptable, like happiness. But, as they learn to trust one another, they will start to share riskier feelings, like sadness, anger, or frustration. When members take greater risks in sharing, and continue to receive care and understanding from other group members, community grows.

Provide a Safe Place for Sharing

To build trust and community in a group, the leader must make sure the group is a safe place to share. Here are some ways you can do this:

Explain and emphasize confidentiality among group members. Make sure that everyone understands how important it is not to repeat to others what group members share with the group. This applies whether the sharing happens during a group meeting or not. Include confidentiality in your group's covenant. Teach about it, model it, and remind group members about it from time to time.

Help group members understand that it is not their place to solve one another's problems, but rather to

---

[2] ChristCare Group Leaders learn extensive community building and leadership skills during their training.

support one another as each wrestles with his or her own problems. When group members know they can share their struggles without others telling them what to do, they are more likely to trust and share.

Create an atmosphere of acceptance in your group, where members value one another for their individuality. Be alert for pressures the group might exert to make members fit a particular mold.

Encourage and affirm group members when they respond in caring ways to one another. As the group establishes a track record in support and care, group members will see it as a place they can share honestly about whatever is going on in their lives.

Make it clear that it's okay to talk about struggles as well as joys. Tell group members very clearly that, "Our group is a place where each of us can feel safe sharing the difficult parts of our lives. God doesn't intend for us to suffer our daily pain alone. He has given us one another. We can listen to and care for one another." Model this attitude in addition to teaching it. For example, when a group member comes to the meeting in tears over a difficult situation, drop your agenda and focus the group's care on that person.

Schedule Sharing Time

Every time your group meets, set aside time for members to tell the group what's been happening in their lives. Then group members will know they always will have a chance to talk about their joys or struggles and receive the group's care and support. The following suggestions can help you structure a constructive and supportive sharing time:

Make sharing voluntary. Never force members to share, and never coerce them into talking about subjects that make them uncomfortable.

Model. Demonstrate the authentic sharing and trust you hope group members will develop. A leader is "a person who goes first." As you share, others will follow your example.

Allow a few minutes at least for each member to share. The more time you allow, the deeper the sharing will be, and the faster your small group's trust, relationships, and community will grow. Of course, the amount of time spent sharing needs to be balanced with other activities. Also, the more members you have, the less time each will have to share.

Be flexible. Allow extra meeting time for sharing, if necessary. This helps when a group member is facing a particularly difficult situation and needs to talk about it.

Encourage sharing at any time. You can expect to see group members sharing about their lives during Biblical Equipping, when praying for one another, while socializing before and after meetings, and in conversations between meetings. In a healthy group, sharing and relationship building is part of everything the group does.

CHAPTER 2

Caring for One Another

As group members trust one another and share more deeply, their opportunities to care for one another will increase. Group members will talk about challenges they face, reveal sorrows in their lives, or discuss changes they want to make. When they do, others in the group will want to respond with care and concern. This care is one of the benefits of belonging to a small group. You don't have to go through difficult times alone, because Jesus is with you always, and so are your fellow group members.

Ways Group Members Care

Group members care for one another in many ways. One of the best is by listening. It's comforting to know that someone is willing to listen and perhaps offer a different perspective on problems. For this reason, group meetings normally include check-in time so that members can listen and respond to others' joy, hurt, sadness, anger, frustration, or losses.

At other times caring takes the form of prayer. Prayer time should be built into each meeting, so that members can pray for one another's challenges and difficulties. The group might also pause in the middle of check-in time to pray for a member's concern that he or she just mentioned.

Group members' care for one another doesn't stop when the group meeting ends. They also care for one another between meetings. This may be as simple as a phone call or a caring note. Between-meetings care could mean keeping a couple's children so the husband and wife can get away together. Even a visit to a lonely group member or an invitation to dinner can express care.

Group members also care for one another during times of crisis. They may help sandbag a members' home threatened by flooding. Some may bring meals to a family with a sick or injured parent. They may visit a hospitalized group member, or drive a group member's children to and from school while he or she is in the hospital.

Simple Rules for Caring

Most of the ways that small group members care for one another are quite simple. They encourage one another, pray for one another, and share one another's joys and sorrows. Groups that observe the following simple rules will successfully care, and will avoid offering care they are not qualified to give.[1]

Listen

Listening means really paying attention, focusing on what the speaker is saying and how he or she says it, and accepting the feelings the speaker expresses. Listening also means not passing judgment, not trying to impose a solution, and not offering meaningless platitudes, such as, "Time heals all wounds," or "Don't worry, everything will be fine."

Take Time

Taking the time to listen is a way of showing care. Depending on the group member's needs, the group may listen for a couple of minutes during check-in time. Other times, you may have to set aside your agenda in order to make enough time to listen to a group member in crisis. Group members can also take time between meetings to call or write a note to a hurting group member.

---

[1] Effective small group care requires well-trained small group leaders. The ChristCare Series provides group leaders with extensive training in Caring in and through Small Groups, Listening, Confidentiality, Making Referrals for Additional Care, Assertiveness, Process-oriented Relating, Dealing with Strong Feelings, as well as many other topics.

Connect with God

Whenever group members offer care, it's important to connect with God, the source of all care. Group members have a responsibility to remind one another of who they are and to whom they belong. They can build one another up with scriptural words of encouragement. They can pray for one another and remind one another of specific ways God has loved and helped them in the past. Group members should always do this for one another, and especially in times of crisis.

Bear One Another's Burdens

Group members care for one another by sharing challenges and pain. This lets hurting group members know that they aren't alone in their troubles—their friends in the small group love them enough to learn about their pain and go through it with them.

Of course, sharing another's pain is not easy. Often people would rather ignore someone else's problems, thinking that they have enough of their own. The group may get uneasy at times when a member shares an uncomfortable situation. But true caring means allowing the hurt person the opportunity to talk openly about troubles or painful experiences. In this way the group shares his or her burden.

Don't Try to Solve Someone Else's Problem

In order to truly care, it's important to realize that you cannot solve others' problems. You can listen, empathize, and pray, but you must let each person find his or her own solutions, with God's help. This is difficult for many people to accept.

Compassionate people are often tempted to fix others' problems. They feel the person's pain so acutely that they want to end it in any way they can. What they must realize is that a hurting person's greatest need is for empathy, not advice. Most people are already aware of ways in which they need to change, and caring friends allow them to do so on their own timetable.

Offer Help

While it's important not to try to solve another

person's problem, it's also important to offer practical help when the other person needs and welcomes it. For example, group members might care for the children of a member whose parent just died, perform maintenance on a group member's car, or help repair a home damaged in a storm. Ideally, group members know that when they are in a crisis they are welcome to call one another—even in the middle of the night—to receive practical and prayerful support.

Don't Try to Carry Too Large a Load of Care

Sometimes small groups try to carry a load of care that is so large that it can destroy the group. This can happen when a group member has a serious long-term need and the group tries to provide all the care he or she needs. This means that the group spends most of its time focusing on that one person's problems, but neglects other group members' needs. The other members may start missing meetings because their needs are no longer being met and may eventually drop out. This may finally cause the group to disband.

Instead of falling into this trap, think about the load of care your group is carrying. Is it too great? If so, consider getting outside help for the person in need, so that the group's own caring resources can be shared more evenly among members.

Get Outside Help When Necessary

One of the biggest mistakes a group leader, or a small group, can make is trying to give care they are not qualified to provide. This happens when one person requires tremendous amounts of care or perhaps professional counseling. When groups try to provide this care, they deprive the hurting person of the care he or she really needs, and they risk hurting the group by neglecting the needs of other members.

As a group leader, you need to be able to recognize when the group is "in over its head."[2] If one group

---

[2] The ChristCare Series trains ChristCare Group Leaders to recognize needs for additional care, and help group members receive enough care, and the right kind of care to meet their needs.

member regularly takes up most of the group's time talking about his or her needs, or if you feel seriously concerned about a group member's well-being, help the group member find additional care from a qualified pastor, counselor, therapist, or physician. Work with your congregation's Equippers[3] (or small group ministry administrators) and your pastor in order to do this.

Does this mean that a person receiving additional care should stop coming to group meetings? Usually not. Typically, the person can still come and receive some care from the group. A professional caregiver with sufficient time and skill will meet the majority of his or her care needs. That way the person receives the care he or she needs, and the group still has time to pay attention to the needs of all its members.

---

[3] Equippers are the pastors and lay leaders who direct ChristCare Group Ministry in their congregations. They correspond to the church staff or lay volunteers who direct small group ministry in congregations without the ChristCare Series.

CHAPTER 3

Incorporating Biblical Equipping into Your Group

Biblical Equipping is the central group activity out of which every other group activity grows. Regularly hearing, reading, and exploring the Bible helps group members understand God's marvelous love for them, what Jesus Christ has done for them, and how they can grow in faith and live as Jesus' more fully committed followers.

David A. Paap, author of *Biblical Equipping: God's Word in Your World*, defines Biblical Equipping this way:

> *Biblical Equipping is a disciplined way of encountering the Bible—by yourself and together with a small group—for the purpose of hearing and understanding God's Word more clearly, knowing and loving God and others more deeply, and living for and serving God more joyfully and obediently.*[1]

Biblical Equipping equips group members to live as Jesus' disciples and to do ministry in his name. Through Biblical Equipping, group members encounter the Scriptures together to discover who God is, how God relates to them, and how they can live according to God's will.

As groups do Biblical Equipping, God's truth, revealed in the Scriptures, begins to mold everything else the group does. It transforms the group's community building and care time—group members use their sharing time to tell one another how the Spirit has

---

[1] David A. Paap, *Biblical Equipping: God's Word in Your World*. (St. Louis: Stephen Ministries, 1996) page 2.

been using the Scriptures to challenge, mold, comfort, change, and bless them. In prayer and worship the group responds to what God has revealed to them in their encounters with the Bible. God's Word directs and empowers group members' service and witness, helping them see what service to give and how to do it.

Characteristics of Biblical Equipping

Following are some of the reasons Biblical Equipping works so well in small groups.

Biblical Equipping is participatory. Everyone in the group participates as they encounter the Bible together. Group members work together to discover the truth about God, themselves, and the world.

The group leader is a facilitator, not a teacher. The leader involves the whole group in thinking about and exploring the meaning of the Bible passage, instead of lecturing to a class of silent students.

The group leader studies the Bible passage ahead of time. Although Biblical Equipping sessions are highly participatory, they are not a theological free-for-all. The group leader learns about the passage ahead of time. He or she identifies difficult passages and learns how to understand them, getting help if necessary. Then at the meeting the group leader acts as a resource for the group—not lecturing on the passage, but sharing information as necessary while group members explore the passage.

The group leader helps the group stay on track theologically. If leaders suspect the group is getting off course theologically, they talk that over with their pastor, their SEA Group[2], or their Equippers or

---

[2] In the ChristCare Series, group leaders provide peer supervision for one another in twice-monthly Support, Encouragement, and Accountability (SEA) Group meetings. They help one another work through challenges in group leadership, pray for one another, and care for one another during difficult times. ChristCare Group Leaders discuss concerns about their groups' Biblical Equipping with their SEA Groups. The SEA Groups work with the ChristCare Group Leaders to help them decide what step to take next with their groups.

small group ministry administrators. Then they lead group members to understandings of biblical teachings that are in line with what their congregation or denomination teaches.

Group members personalize God's truth. As group members learn from and discuss the Scriptures, the leader encourages them to apply biblical truths to their own lives. Biblical Equipping is not just an intellectual exercise. It is a life-changing encounter with the Word of God. Group members discuss what God says and celebrate what God does.

If you want to know more about what Biblical Equipping is and how to lead it, read Rev. Paap's book.[3]

———————————————

[3] ChristCare Group Leaders read *Biblical Equipping: God's Word in Your World* as part of their training. They also receive extensive training in leading Biblical Equipping in their groups. The book and the training combine to thoroughly equip them to lead Biblical Equipping before they ever start leading a ChristCare Group.

CHAPTER 4

Incorporating Prayer and Worship into Your Group

Prayer

Prayer is an important part of every small group's time together. Here are several reasons why. Christ prayed, setting us an example. He commanded his disciples to pray and taught them how.[1] Prayer builds relationships with God. It also helps group members build trust among themselves, as they share their needs for prayer. Learning how to pray better, differently, and more often are other benefits that members receive from group prayer time.

There are many different ways your group can pray. As you lead your group, encourage members to try different types of prayer.

Praying Aloud

Small groups commonly pray aloud. Group members often take turns saying prayers of thanks, praise, or requests to God. These prayers are usually spontaneous—not memorized or pre-planned.

Some groups prefer to take turns praying by moving around the circle. In other groups the members just "jump in" and pray as soon as the previous person stops speaking, regardless of where people are sitting. You can organize the second type of prayer by asking one group member to start and another to close when it seems that everyone who wants to has prayed. Or you yourself might offer to pray last so that you can decide when it's time to stop, sum up with a final prayer, or pray for any request that hasn't yet been covered.

---

[1] Matthew 5:44, 6:9-13; Mark 14:38; Luke 6:28.

How to Teach Group Members to Pray Aloud

In some groups members may be immediately comfortable with praying aloud because they have done so in the past. In this case, you might introduce them to new kinds of prayer with which they are not so familiar. For others who aren't used to it, praying aloud might be frightening or embarrassing at first. In this case, your job is to help group members to become comfortable with praying aloud, but to do this without forcing them. Here are some ways to do that.

Model. If you know or suspect that some members of your small group are uncomfortable praying aloud, set the example by praying aloud yourself. Demonstrate praying in simple, sincere words. The only "out loud" prayers some group members may have heard are very formal prayers read during congregational worship. They may think their prayers need to sound the same way, and worry that they won't measure up. Your example can show them how to talk to God conversationally, as you talk to a trusted friend.

Lead group members one step at a time. If you have group members who are afraid of praying aloud, help them overcome that fear step by step.

- Start by modeling conversational prayer.

- Then ask group members to write out a sentence prayer before the next meeting. Specify the type of prayer (for example, praise or request), then tell group members that you'll ask them to read their prayers aloud at the next meeting.

- After members are comfortable doing this, ask group members to make up short prayers on the spot during group prayer time. You can tell them the week before that you'll be asking them to do this.

- Always make sure group members know they can "pass" if they want to. If group members are jumping in with prayers in no particular order, anyone who wants to pass can just remain silent. When group members are taking turns around the circle, however, passing gets a little bit more involved. Here are several ways they might indicate that they want to pass:

- ◆ by squeezing the hand of the person next to them;

- ◆ by remaining silent for about ten seconds;

- ◆ by simply saying, "Thank you, God."

These small steps, taken slowly, will help most reluctant prayers learn to pray aloud. Once they gain confidence, they will begin to enjoy the group's prayer times.

Singing

Singing is another form of prayer (as well as a way to worship). When we sing to God, we express our prayers in words and music. Music is a second language of love and adoration. Small groups sing prayers of thanksgiving, adoration, and praise.

One strong and willing voice is enough to lead a group in song—no accompaniment is needed. If a group member plays a musical instrument, however, accompaniment can add to your prayerful singing. Your group might enjoy singing time-honored hymns, contemporary songs, or a mixture of both. Group members might also enjoy listening to, or singing along with, tapes or CD's of Christian music.

If you have song sheets for your group, make sure you aren't breaking copyright laws. You can avoid this either by buying song books for your group, or obtaining copyright permission for the songs you copy. There are two organizations that can help you obtain copyright permissions. One is Christian Copyright Licensing, Inc. (CCLI)[2], and the other is LiscenSing.[3] (Check with your church office

---

[2] Christian Copyright Licensing, Inc., 6130 NE 78th Ct., Suite C11, Portland, Oregon 97218-9972; (800) 234-2446.
[3] LiscenSing, Logos Productions Inc., P.O. Box 240, South St. Paul, Minnesota, 55075-0240, (800) 328-0200.

to find out if your congregation already subscribes to one of these services. If not, the congregation's leadership will need to decide whether your congregation will subscribe.)

Other Forms of Prayer

Groups may also pray in silence. Encourage group members to relax and surrender themselves to God. Suggest that they keep their thoughts from wandering by reflecting on the passage they worked with in Biblical Equipping, or by contemplating a question you have asked, such as: "How has God shown love for you?" Or, "How is the Holy Spirit changing you now?" Silent prayer is often difficult, but it can also be refreshing and transforming.

The Christian church has enjoyed prayer litanies and services for centuries. There are many such services, written for different times of day. For instance, *matins* is morning prayer, *vespers* is evening prayer, and *compline* is the last prayer service of night. Check for litanies and prayer services in your congregation's book of worship. Or, if such prayer services are not common in your church, borrow a book of worship from a friend whose congregation uses traditional liturgical worship services.

Prayer Challenges

Group leaders may face some interesting challenges in the area of group prayer. Two of the most common ones are lengthy "epic" prayers, and overly elaborate prayers.

Epic prayers. Sometimes certain group members' prayers seem to go on forever. This causes problems for others who want to pray, and it can cause members' attention to wander. If this occurs in your group, say something like this before each prayer time until the problem resolves itself: "Let's each pray for just a minute or two, so everyone has a chance to pray." Limiting prayer times in this way usually takes care of the problem.

Elaborate prayer. Sometimes a group member will

pray aloud such beautiful or elaborate prayers that he or she intimidates other group members. Members listening to these prayers may compare them with their own simple prayers and conclude that theirs aren't good enough. They may even feel too embarrassed to pray aloud.

If you see this happening, talk privately with those who pray elaborate prayers. Explain to them what you see going on. You can affirm the gifts God has given them, and then ask them to simplify their prayers in order to encourage, not discourage, other group members. As group leader, set an example by modeling short, simple prayers.

Small Group Worship

Many of the psalms give examples of worship. Take a look at Psalm 96 for a picture of what it's like to worship God:

O sing to the LORD a new song;
sing to the LORD, all the earth.
Sing to the LORD, bless his name;
tell of his salvation from day to day.
Declare his glory among the nations,
his marvelous works among all the
peoples.
For great is the LORD, and greatly to be
praised;
he is to be revered above all gods.
For all the gods of the peoples are idols,
but the LORD made the heavens.
Honor and majesty are before him;
strength and beauty are in his sanctuary.

Ascribe to the LORD, O families of the peoples,
ascribe to the LORD glory and strength.
Ascribe to the LORD the glory due his name;
bring an offering, and come into his courts.
Worship the LORD in holy splendor;
tremble before him, all the earth.

Say among the nations, "The LORD is king!
The world is firmly established; it shall
never be moved.
He will judge the peoples with equity"
(Psalm 96:1-10).

You can see from this psalm that worship can take many different forms:

- singing to God;
- remembering the wonderful things God has done;
- blessing God's name;
- telling others how great God is;
- declaring God's glory;
- praising God, his attributes, and his works;
- trembling in God's presence;
- acknowledging God's holiness and greatness;
- bringing an offering to God.

Worship is a proper response to God's greatness, mercy, tender love, and awesome power. It is a way for people to come into God's presence and experience his greatness. Worship is a way Christians love God in return for all the ways God has loved them.

Guidelines for Group Worship

Small group worship is often different from worship with the entire congregation. It is more intimate—the worshippers may be more actively involved. For this reason, group members can experiment with worshipping in different ways. Group leaders can encourage creativity, while ensuring that the worship remains Christ-centered and appropriate for all group members. Here are some suggestions.

Make worship participatory. Get everyone involved in singing, reading Bible passages, sharing their thoughts about a Bible passage, and praying aloud.

Vary the ways you worship. Use a variety of worship

formats. Worship in ways that are familiar to group members, and also in new and different ways. Try focusing worship on different topics, such as thanksgiving for God's blessings or meditating on Jesus' sacrifice. You will get new ideas for worship from the group's regular Biblical Equipping. Talk to other group leaders and learn how their groups worship. Share resources and ideas with one another.

Lead at first, then share the leadership. At first you take responsibility for planning and leading worship. Then share worship responsibilities as soon as group members are ready to take them. Invite group members to bring ideas for worship, to plan the worship portion of the meeting, or to lead worship. Support them in their leadership by providing resources when necessary.

Worship Challenges

You may face some challenges in small group worship. Worship can be very personal, and Christians can be sensitive about their likes and dislikes. Worship is also a way of relating with God, and it is important to direct worship to the one, true God—and not to some substitute.

There may be times when some group members want to worship in a way that makes others in the group uncomfortable. They may wish to use different music or methods of prayer that other members aren't used to or don't find meaningful. This is mainly a matter of personal preference, but it can lead to conflict as group members try to defend their ideas of the "right" way to worship.

When group members consider their own rights more important than others', help them to step back and focus less on their rights—and focus more on love. This might be a good opportunity to study 1 Corinthians 8:1-13. In this passage, you read that some Christians ate meat from animals that had been sacrificed at pagan temples. (After the animals were sacrificed, the meat was sold to the public. As far as these Christians were concerned, they weren't going to a pagan temple, they were buying meat from a local butcher.) Other Christians said eating meat from those animals was the same as worshipping the idols to which the animals had been sacrificed. Paul recommended that neither side insist on their rights. Instead, Paul encouraged them to give up their rights out of love for their brothers and sisters. Paul said that, in such cases, loving one another was even more important than having the correct opinions.

If members disagree about worship, encourage them to discuss what's going on—to bring the disagreement out in the open. Then encourage them to put love first, making compromises that can meet everyone's needs. Group members who are enthusiastic about making changes in the group's worship style may need to go more slowly for the sake of others, allowing them to get used to the new ways. The group may also continue to use specific elements of worship that certain group members love and find especially meaningful. Conversely, group members who resist change need to stretch, to be willing to experiment, and to accept some new ways of worshipping, out of Christian love for those members who find new and different worship styles more meaningful.

Remember that disagreements of this sort can be part of the group's struggle to build community. They can be frustrating and difficult to work through, but the process of discussing and resolving them can have great benefits, both for the quality of your group's worship, and for your experience of Christian community.

A group member may want to lead the group in non-Christian worship, such as worship of a Native American "Great Spirit," or another deity. He or she may believe that all worship is basically the same—

that all worship is directed toward God, whatever you call him. The first commandment and many other passages in Scripture make it clear that this is not true.

If this occurs in your group, you need to speak privately with the person. You could look at Exodus 20:1-6 together and discuss the important connection between trusting and believing in God and worshipping him. Gently but clearly say that in this group, worship will be directed only toward the true God that Jesus revealed. This can become a point of clarification, not division. Regardless of the discussion's outcome, you are responsible for ensuring that only Christian worship occurs in your group. You may want to seek the help of your pastor, SEA Group, Equipper, or small group ministry administrator if a problem like this comes up in your group.

CHAPTER 5

Helping Your Group Serve

The fourth main activity in small groups is missional service. Missional service means reaching out with Christ's love to those outside the small group. God has given a great deal to group members: the understanding and support of other group members; a place to belong; a place to encounter the Scriptures, pray, and worship together; and a place to grow in Jesus. Grateful group members don't hoard God's gifts, saving them only for one another. Instead, they follow Jesus into missional service.

The last time Jesus and his disciples were together before he was crucified, he knelt before them and washed their feet. Here's what happened next:

> After he had washed their feet, had put on his robe, and had returned to the table, he said to them, "Do you know what I have done to you? You call me Teacher and Lord—and you are right, for that is what I am. So if I, your Lord and Teacher, have washed your feet, you also ought to wash one another's feet. For I have set you an example, that you also should do as I have done to you. Very truly, I tell you, servants are not greater than their master, nor are messengers greater than the one who sent them. If you know these things, you are blessed if you do them" (John 13:12-17).

To be a Christian, then, is to be a servant. *Christian* means *Christ-like*. Since serving is one aspect of being Christ-like, small groups that are Christian will perform missional service.

As a small group leader, one of your most important jobs is to help your group become and remain missional. A group is not healthy if it is focused solely on itself. Group members who realize this will find ways to serve others. This ensures that the group stays Christian and continues to thrive spiritually.

There are several important responsibilities small group leaders have as they lead their groups into missional service:

- instilling missional values;
- helping the group grow into service;
- offering choices;
- making sure the group stays missional.

Instilling Missional Values

Group members live according to what they believe is most important. If they believe that the group exists only for them, they will act as if it does. But if they believe that Jesus is calling the group to serve, their actions will show that belief.

Part of the small group leader's job is to help group members hear Christ's call to service and understand that it is a call to *them*— that God is counting on them to serve. Then, with the Spirit's inspiration and power, group members can overcome their natural tendency to focus only on themselves, and follow Jesus instead.

Model Servanthood

You can model servanthood in several ways. As a servant leader, your goal is to help others grow and achieve their goals. Servant leaders take charge when they need to, but they are also willing to take the most difficult or least glorious jobs for themselves. Servant leaders care more about the feelings, thoughts, and well-being of group members than about how many projects the group completes or how many workbooks they finish. To sum up, servant leaders do not lead in order to serve their own desires, but rather to serve God, their fellow group members, and those God puts in their path.

Talk about Missional Service

From the beginning of your group's life, you should talk about its purpose: to serve God and others. When your group establishes its covenant, lead group members to commit the group to Jesus' service. Whenever your group chooses the topic for a new Biblical Equipping series, encourage them to choose one that leads to missional service. Whenever group members evaluate where the group has been and where it is going, ask, "Are we serving, and growing toward greater missional service?" In short, whenever group members make decisions about group activities, help them ask the question, "How will this activity help us serve more effectively?"

Helping the Group Grow into Missional Service

It's a fact that group members who have gained some Christian maturity are more likely to serve others than those who are less mature. There are several ways you can help group members grow and mature.

Focus on Group Members' Growth

Realize that some group members may need to spend time focusing on themselves and their own needs before they are ready to serve. For example, think of a new group mostly made up of people who have recently resumed attending church after years of inactivity. They have joined a small group with others with similar experiences so that they can work together to make sense of their experiences and rediscover what it means to be part of the church.

Members of this group would need to spend time telling their own stories. They would need time to learn to trust both one another and the church. If their group leader pushed them too soon to set aside their own needs and focus on mission, probably it would bring back times in the past when they believed church members were trying to use them instead of caring for them. They aren't ready for reaching out in mission yet. Instead, the leader of such a group would need to teach members to serve by first serving them.

If you lead a group that needs to devote some time to its own growth and healing, help members understand that it is only for a limited period. They are focusing on their own growth now so they can become more effective missional servants later. Help group members catch the vision of all God's people as missional servants. Then at some point you will say, "We have focused inward long enough. Now we need to turn our focus outward for awhile."

Equip Group Members Biblically

Group members also grow into mission through their encounters with the Scriptures. For example, they learn from the Bible that God blesses people so that they can be a blessing to others. They see Jesus' example, who gave himself for others. They hear and explore passages that describe how Jesus' followers gave themselves completely to God so that others could know the Good News about Jesus.

The Holy Spirit uses the Scriptures to bring group members to maturity and to increase their faith. Missional service will become second nature as group members become more familiar with the Bible and God's Word takes root in their lives.

Don't Be Afraid to Challenge

Some small groups never move into mission. These groups may have started with an inward focus and never got around to changing it. Perhaps the importance of mission wasn't made clear to them early on. Members of such groups may say things like, "If we allow others into our group, we won't be able to share as deeply," or "We're so busy caring for one another, we just don't have time to reach out to others," or even, "This group has come to mean so much to us, let's not do anything to change it now."

Group members need to learn that such attitudes will destroy the group they have come to value so highly. If a group stops growing—not only in numbers, but also in faith and discipleship—it dies. If group members don't reach out, they have nothing to bring back into the group. Small groups must serve if they want to thrive.

Offering Choices

Group leaders help members choose how to serve, and one good way to do this is to offer the group a variety of choices. Instead of saying, "Do you want to serve?" say, "Shall we serve in this way or that way; or do you have better ideas?" Treat service as a given, and focus the group's discussion on the kind of service God is leading them into, based on their gifts, interests, and availability.

Be sure you don't push the small group into service that is far above their abilities and availability. If the group doesn't succeed, members will become discouraged and less likely to try missional service again. At the same time, it's important to find service that is challenging to group members. Otherwise they may become bored and lose interest.

Types of Missional Service

There are many types of missional service. Every group should be able to find a project that fits its members' gifts and interests.

Evangelism

A small group can be a very effective setting for evangelism. People who wouldn't darken the door of a church might come to a group meeting if a friend invites them. Once they come to the meeting, group members can demonstrate Christ's love by listening, caring, paying attention to guests' needs, and relating in accepting, loving, nonjudgmental ways. As group members pray and discuss the Scriptures together, nonChristian guests may see Jesus at the center of their group. By talking about how God makes a difference in their lives, group members witness to non-Christians who experience similar life challenges and also need God's care and help.

Of course, groups pay a price for evangelistically welcoming visitors and new members. It *does* disrupt the group's community and cohesiveness when new-comers are there. Group members may feel less free to share their deeply-felt needs and challenges. The group has to adjust to new personalities. Group members may grieve for the loss of the group as it was before the new members joined. In fact, if the group grows too large, it will even need to subdivide, with some original members in each new group.

Groups need vision and commitment to Jesus to accept such challenges. Yet many groups accept the challenges and serve evangelistically because they want others to experience God's blessings, just as they have.

Ministry to Wholistic Needs

God created people with a set of interrelated needs: not only spiritual needs, but also physical, social, intellectual, and emotional needs. Some groups focus their missional service on meeting these wholis-tic needs. For instance, group members might work together at a food pantry, visit and pray with residents at extended care facilities, or rehabilitate houses for homeless people. They might tackle one-time projects together, such as cleaning a park or a stream, or pro-viding summer recreational opportunities for under-privileged children. All of these meet wholistic needs.

Intercessory Prayer

Some groups do missional service by praying for people outside the group, both at meetings and between meetings. They learn of others' needs and bring them to the group for prayer, being careful not to reveal identities or other confidential information. Between group meetings they continue praying and sharing needs. Members of such groups sacrifice their time and energy to intercede for others.

Building Disciples

Some congregations use small groups to help members grow as more deeply committed disciples so they eventually become more effective congregation leaders. These groups' mission is focused inward on group members—challenging them, holding them accountable, nurturing, teaching, and building them up in Christian discipleship. Yet the inward focus is not selfish, for it is aimed toward future ministry. The group members know that the intense attention they are receiving now is intended to prepare them to serve Jesus and their congregation in the months and years to come.

Supporting Group Members in Missional Activities

Some groups have members who perform different kinds of missional service on an individual basis. Some may be daily-life evangelists reaching out with Christ's love to friends, coworkers, and neighbors; others may serve as teachers in the Sunday School, or volunteers at the local food pantry; still others may be full-time Christian workers. The group serves by supporting its members whenever the going gets tough, and by encouraging one another and holding one another accountable for continuing service. Group members come up with new ideas for service, help one another discover and develop their Spirit-given gifts, and find new ways for members to use their gifts.

Members of such a group may occasionally do missional service projects together. Usually, however, their primary missional service is supporting members in individual service outside the group.

Making Sure the Group Stays Missional

There are several things you can do to help the group stay missional. Sometimes groups can drift away from missional service without noticing. If this happens, the leader is responsible for bringing the group back to its original purpose of serving God and one another.

Group leaders should also help their groups recovenant every six months. That means that twice a year the groups evaluate both *what* they've been doing and *how* they've been doing. When your group members evaluate themselves, always encourage them to think about the service they're involved in or the mission they're preparing for.[1]

As you help your group stay missional, you aren't doing it on your own. The Holy Spirit himself will continue to work in group members' lives, transforming them into Jesus' more fully devoted followers. People who are being changed into the image of Jesus will naturally serve as he did.

---

[1] If you are a ChristCare Group Leader, the "Recovenanting Form" (see Appendix A of module II.H., How to Bring Closure to ChristCare Groups) will remind you to do this.

CHAPTER 6

Choosing a Special Emphasis for Your Group

Every small group needs to include all four small group activities: community building and care, Biblical Equipping, prayer and worship, and missional service. Some groups, however, will consistently emphasize one activity more than others in order to serve Jesus. Following are some of the special emphases small groups might have.

Possible Group Emphases

Biblical Equipping

This group makes digging into the Bible its top priority. Members might spend two-thirds of the meeting time in hearing, exploring, and applying a portion of the Bible. The group's purpose is to help members grow in faith and obedience through concentrated exposure to God's Word.

Intercessory Prayer

People sometimes join a group in order to pray for others. When they meet they tell of their own and others' needs for prayer, and then spend a lot of time praying together for those needs. This becomes their primary form of service.

Evangelism

Members of groups with an evangelism emphasis encourage one another to invite others to the group— friends, neighbors, and co-workers, especially non-Christians. These groups choose their activities based on the needs of guests who may know little about church or the Bible. They spend their meeting time on simple Biblical Equipping, community building, and caring. They witness about the effect Jesus has in their lives. Since evangelistic groups must eventually subdivide due to growth, such groups also concentrate on developing new leaders.

Accountability

People sometimes join groups in order to hold one another accountable for growing and living as Jesus' disciples. Members of such groups often agree to meet together for a year or more. Then at their meetings they concentrate intensively on Biblical Equipping and prayer. They share deeply and honestly about their successes and failures in trying to live as Jesus' fully devoted followers. They often agree to practice daily spiritual disciplines.

Service

Sometimes Christians join together in small groups in order to perform a single special service such as working in a food pantry, providing child care, or singing in the choir. Members of such groups spend most of their time in their chosen service, but they also pray together, do Biblical Equipping together, and support one another by listening and caring. Groups like this keep people from "ministry burn-out," since group members care and support one another, and build their ministry on a strong foundation of prayer and Scripture.

Ministry Support

People involved in different ministries might form groups to support one another. Sometimes their ministries are similar—teaching Sunday School or living as daily-life evangelists. Other times, the ministries are diverse, for example, serving at a homeless shelter, working on the church staff, or leading a youth group. These people meet together, share about their ministries, pray and care for one another, and encounter the Scriptures to seek God's guidance for their service.

Balanced Group

Some groups will not emphasize any of the four

group activities. These groups will balance all four activities, do missional service through regular projects, and provide a consistent environment in which group members care for one another and help one another grow as disciples.

How Groups with Different Emphases Use Their Time

The chart on page 35 shows how small groups with different emphases might use their time. Notice that all the groups include all four small group activities—community building and care, Biblical Equipping, prayer and worship, and missional service—even though they emphasize one. Each group in the example meets for 90 minutes. Of course, your group's meetings may be longer or shorter.

What Will *Your* Group's Emphasis Be?

Groups can have many different emphases, and one group's emphasis may change over time. There are several factors that may go into choosing a group's emphasis.

Congregational Directives

Many congregations have very specific missions for their small groups, such as evangelism, new member assimilation, or leadership development. In such a case, your group may be assigned an emphasis that carries out the congregation's mission.

Members' and Leader's Mutual Choice

Some small groups begin without a clear mission, and group members may have no previous group experience. In this case, it's best to give members a chance to experience all four typical group activities, and try different kinds of missional service. Then, when the group has been going for awhile, members and leader may decide they want to emphasize one of the activities in order to carry out their mission.

How Small Groups with Different Emphases Use Meeting Time

BIBLICAL EQUIPPING-EMPHASIS GROUP

Biblical Equipping...50-60 min.
Community Building and Care, Prayer and Worship,
 Missional Service..30-40 min.

PRAYER-EMPHASIS GROUP

Prayer and Worship...45 min.
Biblical Equipping...25 min.
Community Building and Care....................................20 min.
Missional Service=Prayer

EVANGELISM-EMPHASIS GROUP

Community Building and Care.............................45-55 min.
Biblical Equipping, Prayer and Worship...............35-45 min.
Missional Service=Evangelism

ACCOUNTABILITY-EMPHASIS GROUP

Biblical Equipping, Prayer and Worship....................50 min.
Community Building and Care ....40 min.
Missional Service=Growing as disciples to prepare for service

SERVICE-EMPHASIS GROUP

Community Building and Care, Biblical Equipping,
 Prayer and Worship ....30 min.
Missional Service ....60 min.

MINISTRY SUPPORT GROUP

Community Building and Care ....45 min.
Biblical Equipping, Prayer and Worship....................45 min.
Missional Service=Individual Ministries

BALANCED GROUP

Community Building and Care ....30 min.
Biblical Equipping...45 min.
Prayer and Worship...15 min.
Missional Service=Regular Projects

Changing Circumstances

A healthy small group is changing, not static. The group may change from one emphasis to another as it matures. For instance, a group that has met together for a couple years may decide it's ready to reach out to others by dividing into two groups and inviting new members. Or, group members who have discovered their spiritual gifts of prayer may decide to become a group that strongly emphasizes intercession. Since groups change over time, one of the advantages of recovenanting every six months is that group members are free then to reconsider their group's emphasis.

Always Missional

Decisions about group emphasis are mission-driven. Ask: What is the best way for this group to accomplish God's purpose for it? Is it through prayer? Community building? A combination of both? Something else?

As you help your group determine its identity, always bring members back to the most important question: How can we best serve Jesus?

CHAPTER 7

Realizing the Effects of Group Size

While small groups may be as small as three members or as large as twelve, the ideal size is five to ten members. This size has many advantages.

Groups with five to ten members have all the advantages of smallness.

- They have plenty of time at each meeting for each group member to get involved in sharing, prayer, and discussion.

- Quiet people don't feel overlooked or left out.

- Since group members have more time for sharing, they build a sense of community quickly.

- There's "growing room" in a group of that size. The group can continue to welcome new members until it reaches twelve. Then the group will need to divide into two new groups.

When groups have more than twelve members community starts to break down. There's less time for each person to share or participate in group discussions. That's why it's much better to divide a large group when it reaches twelve members, thus keeping the advantages of being small.

It's usually not a good idea for small groups to go below five members. In a group that small, when one or two members are absent, it leaves a tremendous gap. The only time you might consider starting with three or four group members would be if you have an evangelistic group that is dedicated to growing very rapidly.

CHAPTER 8

Deciding Whether to Be Open or Closed

Open and Closed Groups

Open Groups

Groups that are "open" reach out with God's love by regularly inviting and welcoming visitors and new members. Such groups can grow quickly. When groups have ten or more regularly attending members, they should immediately begin making plans to divide into two groups and begin the growing process again.

Closed Groups

Groups that are "closed" restrict their membership to a certain number. After they reach that number, they no longer actively invite visitors to group meetings. This allows them to focus more deeply on members' needs, and on building relationships— among members and with God. Although their membership is closed, these groups still do missional service for others outside the group. They may serve through special projects, or by supporting one another in daily life evangelism or other forms of individual service.

The chart on the next page compares open and closed groups.

Deciding Whether to Be Open or Closed

There are several factors that influence a small group's decision on whether to be open or closed.

Type of Group

Some types of groups are open or closed by definition. Evangelism-emphasis groups must be open to continue growing and dividing. Accountability-emphasis groups are usually closed because of the deep levels of honesty and sharing they require. Other types of groups, such as prayer-emphasis or Biblical Equipping-emphasis groups, can be either open or closed, depending on the needs and comfort levels of group members.

Characteristics of Open and Closed Groups

Open Groups	Groups
Always welcome guests and new members	Do not seek guests or new members
Actively and regularly reach out to include others in the group	Build deep levels of community and trust among existing group members
Often keep personal sharing and Bible discussions simple to accommodate new group members and new Christians	Promote in-depth learning
Can reach many people with Christian care, especially people who aren't actively involved in a congregation	Focus on a few people in order to help them grow into more effective servants
Enable more people—church members and nonmembers—to experience the benefits of small groups	Foster honesty and high accountability among group members
Often experience fast growth in group membership	Enable group members to grow more deeply in their relationships with God and with one another
Contribute to overall growth in the congregation's membership and discipleship	Contribute mature lay leaders and more fully devoted disciples

The Group's Changing Needs

As open groups grow and mature, or as members go through life crises, they may want to close the group temporarily. This allows deeper community building or ministering to group members. Conversely, closed groups may decide to become open in order to expand and grow, thus fulfilling their needs for mission.

Avoid Self-Centered Reasons

Group leaders should be aware that groups can decide to be either open or closed for the wrong reasons. A group could decide to be open in order to avoid deep sharing and community building. Members of such a group may be reluctant to move past surface issues and challenge one another to grow. On the other hand, a group could decide to be closed in order to avoid reaching out to others. Group members may become too comfortable in a closed group and decide that they don't want to be bothered with missional service. Group leaders try to help groups find better reasons than these when deciding whether to be open or closed.

Always Missional

Choosing to be open or closed, just like choosing an emphasis, is a mission-driven decision.

There may be missional reasons to be a closed group. If your group's mission is to become the best disciples possible, and if that can be done only in a closed setting, then it is appropriate for the group to close. Yet such a group will always keep in mind that Jesus sends his disciples into mission and will take seriously its mission to others outside the group. Again, if a group is taking on an especially challenging service project and needs to maintain close working relationships, it might be best to be a closed group. Even a large, newly-formed group might need to focus on building community and therefore choose to close temporarily, opening later when group members are prepared to welcome new members and grow further.

Small groups without a valid missional reason to be closed will remain open. This is because one major missional purpose of open groups is to include new members, thus fulfilling Christ's Great Commission: "Go therefore and make disciples of all nations. . ." (Matthew 28:19).

PART TWO

Deciding Where, When, and How Long to Meet

A small group's life together revolves around regular group meetings. The choices you and your group make about group meetings will affect your group in several very important ways. These choices will help determine:

- who will be able to participate in your group;
- how quickly your group will develop trusting community;
- the roles various group members will play in the group;
- what your group's mission will be; and
- how well your group will carry out its mission.

Part Two of this book lays out the choices you and your group will make, and explains what effects those choices will probably have.

CHAPTER 9

Choosing a Meeting Place

One of the first decisions you'll need to make about your small group is where to meet. A good meeting place provides atmosphere, convenience, safety, seating, comfort, and other elements necessary for successful group meetings. A poor meeting place can so distract from the purpose and content of the meeting that it ruins all the hard work you've done to gather the group members and plan the meeting.

What to Look for in a Meeting Location

Use the following checklist to evaluate possible meeting places for your group.

Location Checklist

❑ A reasonable distance from group members' homes

❑ Adequate and safe parking nearby

❑ Space large enough for members to sit in a circle (so everyone can see and hear everyone else)

❑ Comfortable seating

❑ Adequate light, heat, and air conditioning

❑ Easily accessible rest room

❑ Telephone available (for emergency calls)

❑ Quiet, private, pleasant atmosphere

❑ Insurance coverage in case of accidents

When searching for a meeting space, you will also want to consider any special needs your group members may have.

Special Requirements Checklist

❏ *Group members' health problems.* Is anyone allergic to pets? Is anyone unable to climb stairs? Are any group members in wheelchairs? If so, are the rest room and the meeting room accessible?

❏ *Storage.* Will you need storage space for extra Bibles, songbooks, or study materials?

❏ *Seating.* Do any group members have physical problems requiring special seating?

❏ *Accessibility.* Do any group members have disabilities that require ramps, accessible rest rooms, or other special arrangements?

❏ *Smoking.* If your group permits smoking, will your location allow it? Do any group members have physical conditions that make it difficult for them to meet in a place where smoking is permitted, even if no one smokes during the meeting?

❏ *Refreshment facilities.* Do you need to use kitchen facilities to keep or prepare refreshments?

❏ *Child-care facilities.* Do you plan to provide child care during your group meetings? If so, you'll need a separate area for the children.

Meeting at Church

One possible location for small group meetings is a room in your church. There are many advantages to this. Everyone knows how to get there, and the distance from group members' homes is usually reasonable. The many small details—lighting, rest rooms, handicapped accessibility, storage space—may be already taken care of. Group members don't have to spend time preparing their homes to host meetings. Nor do they have to worry about the effect on other family members, keeping pets out of the way, or dealing with unexpected visitors or phone calls during the meeting.

Yet while church rooms may seem to be ideal meeting places, they do have drawbacks. The rooms are usually not as friendly and inviting as those in a home, which may mean that it will take your group longer to get comfortable and build community. Room set-up and take-down may be difficult, and seating is often not be as comfortable as it would be in a home. Phones, rest rooms, and kitchens may be inconvenient or locked at the time your group meets. You may need to reserve the meeting room, and there may be scheduling conflicts.

Making the Most of a Church Meeting Room

Here are some tips if you decide that a church meeting room is best for your group.

Choose the room carefully. A lounge area with comfortable seating and privacy can provide a friendly atmosphere for small groups. If such a room isn't available, a classroom or section of a larger room can work. Make sure you can reserve the room on a long-term basis; frequent room changes will disrupt your group's continuity. If you will meet in a church classroom, see if you can bring a lamp, a tablecloth, or other items that will make the room feel more comfortable.

Make a large space intimate. If you must use a large room (such as a gymnasium), you may want to switch off the overhead lights and use floor lamps or table lamps to light the area your group will use. The small, warm circles of light will create an intimate atmosphere. Place chairs in a circle, close together, to define the group's space. Dividers or partitions can also help define a smaller space. Several small groups can meet in a large room simultaneously using this set-up.

Request facilities in advance. If your group plans to use the kitchen, check the church schedule and get permission ahead of time. Find out about, and follow, the usage, clean-up, and security procedures.

Plan for emergencies. If telephone access is difficult, ask group members to consider investing in an electronic pager (or "beeper"). If a group member already has a beeper or cellular phone, ask if he or she is willing to let the group give baby-sitters and family members the number for emergency calls during meetings.

Meeting in a Home

A home can offer a warm, intimate, and comfortable setting—an atmosphere conducive to good community building. In a home, usually your problems of kitchen, rest room, and telephone access are solved. Moreover, if you meet at the same home every time, you have the advantages of members always knowing where the meeting is, and perhaps of being able to store supplies on-site. For these reasons, meeting in a home is often the best choice for a group.

But there also may be disadvantages to meeting in a member's home. Parking may be a problem. Neighbors may not appreciate cars taking over their personal parking spaces, or maybe even blocking their driveways. There may not be enough outside lighting for group members to feel safe walking to and from their cars, especially in an unsafe neighborhood.

Other possible disadvantages to meeting in a home deal mostly with available space. The home may not have a room large enough for group members to sit facing one another in a circle. (Good community building requires that everyone be able to see and hear everyone else.) Additionally, many homes have steps and narrow doors, making it difficult or impossible for some persons with disabilities to attend.

Making the Most of Meeting in a Home

If you do decide to meet in a home, here are some things you can do to make the most of this location.

Plan ahead to keep interruptions to a minimum. Ask the host to make sure other family members won't disturb the meeting by playing music or television loudly.

Decide ahead of time how to handle phone calls. It's best if a member of the host's family (who is not a member of the group) can screen calls, interrupting the group only for emergencies. If that's impossible, perhaps the host can sit in a place that allows him or her to slip out and go to another room. That way, he or she can answer the phone or screen a call on the answering machine without disturbing the rest of the group. If you use an answering machine, you could create a special tape for use during meetings that says something like, "Thanks for calling. We are holding a small group meeting in our home right now. If this is an emergency, please say so and we will pick up the phone. Otherwise, please leave a message. We will call you back later."

Let the host take responsibility for answering the door. This way, he or she can make arrangements to talk with an unexpected guest later, or even invite the guest to join the meeting if it's an open group.

Make arrangements for pets. Pets might interrupt the meeting or set off group members' allergies. It is probably better to ask the host to keep pets outdoors or in another part of the house.

When the Meeting Rotates between Several Homes

Rotating group meetings among members' homes spreads out the responsibilities that come with hosting. If you choose this alternative, here are some ideas you'll want to consider to make it work smoothly.

Use the checklist above. Do this for every home your group uses. Based on your findings, you may want to rotate among two or three members' homes rather than use all of them. Just keep in mind that homes that can't accommodate group meetings might still work for parties or mission projects.

Announce the location. Make sure all group members and potential guests know where your group is meeting. Use bulletin announcements, printed schedules, postcard reminders, and phone calls to regular guests or absent group members.

Directions. Be sure all group members and regular guests have directions or maps to each meeting location.

Missional Considerations

Your choice of meeting place will certainly affect your group's mission. For example, an evangelism-emphasis group is often much more effective meeting in a home rather than at the church, since non-churched people are much more likely to accept an invitation into a home. You may even want to hold the group meetings in a neighborhood you've chosen to evangelize. This makes the meeting as convenient as possible for the people you want to reach.

An evangelism-emphasis group will also be more effective if it always meets at the same time and place. That way occasional guests can always find the group meeting when they want to attend. Similar logic applies to the question of how frequently to meet. A group emphasizing evangelism may choose to meet every week so that guests don't get confused about when the group meets and accidentally show up for a meeting during the wrong week.

Other mission emphases may require other choices about where to meet. For example, a prayer-emphasis group will put more of a premium on a quiet meeting place with no interruptions than will an evangelism-emphasis group that reaches out to parents of young children. A service-emphasis group may meet at the homeless shelter where they serve.

Christian small groups exist to serve Jesus. Your choices about meeting place will reflect your reason for existence.

CHAPTER 10

Choosing a Meeting Time

Choosing a meeting time sounds simple, but there are many factors to consider. Work, family, and church schedules are just a few. Listed below are some ideas for possible meeting times.

Possible Meeting Times

Weekday Evenings

Weekday evenings may work well for group members with typical daytime jobs. 7 p.m. is often the earliest workable starting time, and 10 p.m. is about the latest you'll want to end a weeknight group. If group members report to work early or have to take sitters home, you may need to end at 9:00 or 9:30.

Weekday Mornings or Afternoons

For groups with members who can arrange their own schedules, who work evenings or nights, or who do not work outside their homes, mornings and afternoons can be ideal meeting times. Retired persons and parents with children in school may especially appreciate meeting during the day.

Weekdays before Work

This can be a good time for group members who can leave home early enough to meet for an hour before going to work or starting their day at home. Some groups that meet at this time combine breakfast with their meeting, either in a group member's home, or in a restaurant with a private area. Since group members probably have to be at work at a specific time, it's extremely important to begin and end meetings on time.

Weekday Lunch Hours

Small groups of coworkers or students frequently choose this meeting time. These groups often meet weekly, or even more frequently, to make up for their limited time together.

Saturdays

Groups whose members live far apart, or who are just too busy to meet during the week, may set aside time on Saturdays.

Sundays before or after Worship Services

This saves a trip for groups who meet in church facilities, but finding meeting space can be a challenge. In addition, people who have responsibilities during worship or Sunday School may be very tired by the time the group meeting begins.

Sunday Afternoons or Evenings

Busy people are often free at these times, but a group may have to compete with recreational activities.

Times Not to Meet

You and your group also need to consider times that meetings should not be scheduled. These include:

- nights when church services, or other major congregational events, are regularly scheduled, (for example, some congregations hold regular Wednesday night services);

- times when popular community activities (such as high school sports events or community concerts) are regularly scheduled.

Deciding When to Meet

There are several ways to decide when your group will meet.

- As group leader, you may select the meeting time based on your schedule, before any members join the group. This then becomes a major factor in finding group members—only those who can meet at the time you've chosen will consider joining the group.

- You may set a time for the initial meeting, and then let the group members who come decide together on the time that the group will regularly meet.

- Your congregation may choose to have all small groups meet at the same time. This has the disadvantage of limiting participation to those who have that one night free for meetings.

If You Can't Find a Time That Works for Everyone

Occasionally a small group will not be able to find a time that works for everyone who initially signed up. The majority of group members may choose a time that doesn't work for a few others. This can result in hurt feelings. Someone who can only meet on a particular night may feel left out if the group chooses a different night. In such a case, do everything you can to alleviate hurt feelings and help those who can't meet at the designated time find another group to join.

Another option is to divide the original group into two groups that meet at different times. This is possible only if another small group leader is available and if the original group is large enough to divide.

CHAPTER 11

Meeting Frequency

Small groups may meet once a week, twice a month, or once a month.

Factors That Influence How Often Groups Meet

There are many factors that go into the decision of how often to meet. Your group may need to take several of these into account.

The Group's Mission

The first factor is how often your group needs to meet in order to accomplish your mission. For example, a service-emphasis group that helps serve meals at a homeless shelter twice a month, needs to meet at least twice a month at the shelter. A different example is a prayer-emphasis group committed to responding to congregation members' prayer requests, which may need to meet once a week.

Meeting Length

Some groups that meet for two hours may meet less frequently. Groups with meetings shorter than 90 minutes will probably meet once a week. Groups that have 90 minute meetings may meet once a week or twice a month.

How Often Members Can Meet

The busier people's lives are, the less time they have available for group meetings. Some groups, however, choose to meet once a week, in spite of their busy lives, because members need and enjoy the benefits of very frequent group meetings.

Direction from Your Congregation

Congregations may recommend or require a particular frequency for small group meetings.

Advantages to Meeting Once a Week

When small groups meet once a week they receive many benefits, such as the following:

Community Building. A group that meets weekly is likely to build community faster, and bond more deeply, than groups that meet less frequently.

Habit. People get into the habit of setting aside the same time every week for their small group meeting. They never have to wonder about the date of the next meeting. If members need to miss a meeting for some reason, it's only a week until the next one—they don't have time to get out of the habit of attending.

Continuity. Whether group members are working through a book of the Bible, doing a service project, or discussing the basics of Christian life, they're less likely to forget what they've learned between meetings. Group members find it easier to stay up to date on what's happening in other group members' lives.

Commitment and Accountability. If group members have assignments between meetings, such as inviting others to group meetings or reading portions of Scripture, study guides, or books, they are less likely to put the job off when they only have a week to get it done.

Outreach. Visitors who haven't attended for a while and then want to come back don't have to wonder if there's a meeting this week.

Disadvantages to Meeting Once a Week

Of course, there are also some disadvantages to meeting weekly.

Time Constraints. Busy people may be less willing to make a weekly commitment, resulting in fewer people who want to join the group.

Extra Preparation. Weekly meetings are more work for the small group leader and others in the group who take active leadership roles.

Schedule Conflicts. Weekly meetings may conflict more often with group members' other responsibilities.

Advantages to Meeting Twice a Month

Scheduling small group meetings twice a month has many advantages for the average group.

Community Building. Meeting twice a month is frequent enough for most groups to build a solid sense of community. The level of trust probably won't equal that of once-a-week groups, but it is certainly sufficient for carrying out the four basic group activities.

Busy Schedules. People with busy schedules and heavy commitments can fit in twice-a-month group meetings more easily. This means you may have more people interested in joining the group.

Child (or Other Family Member) Care. Group members who need to hire baby sitters may find it easier and less expensive to do so only twice a month. Members who care for disabled or elderly relatives may also appreciate having to make arrangements less often.

Preparation Time. The small group leader and others in group leadership roles have more time to prepare between meetings, which can be a help. Group members may also appreciate having extra time to complete assignments or projects.

Disadvantages to Meeting Twice a Month

Deep Community Building. Since there is simply less time spent together, group members miss out on some of the concentrated community building that can happen with weekly meetings.

Scheduling. Members may have difficulty remembering which weeks contain group meetings, particularly if they have recently missed a meeting. This can also be a problem for visitors.

Reasons That Groups Meet Monthly

Occasionally, small groups work best if they meet monthly. Here are some reasons.

Vacations. Some groups adopt a temporary monthly schedule during the summer vacation period. This enables the group to maintain a sense of community so that, in September, it can quickly pick up where it left off.

Closure. A group might adopt a monthly schedule near the end of its life as a way of winding down. If it is planning to divide into two new groups, however, continuing to meet weekly or bimonthly will help maintain momentum during the transition period.

Tasks. Some groups focus on mission or service projects, such as visiting nursing homes or distributing food to the homeless. These groups might find that once a month is best for these activities.

Disadvantages of Meeting Once a Month

Difficult Community Building. Monthly meetings don't allow enough contact among members for them to be able to share deeply and develop trust. For this reason, community building becomes very difficult.

Scheduling. Meeting monthly makes it harder for members and visitors to remember meeting dates.

Attendance. If a member must miss a meeting, he or she will have to wait a month for the next one and may easily get out of the habit of attending. Missing two months (due to illness, schedule conflicts, or a combination of reasons) can leave a member so out of touch with the rest of the group that he or she no longer feels comfortable in the meeting.

CHAPTER 12

Setting a Meeting Length

How long should your group meet? Meetings may be as short as an hour or less, or as long as over two hours. You need to think carefully when you plan how long your meeting will be. Otherwise, you could run into problems like these:

- your group may lose members because every meeting goes on for three hours; or

- your group will never accomplish its mission because you never spend enough time together to do so.

Factors to Consider in Setting a Meeting Length

The best length for a small group meeting depends on the group's mission and activities. Here are some factors to take into account.

The Group's Mission

How long will it take to carry out the group's mission? A weekly group that supports members in their individual service may only need to meet for an hour to fulfill its mission. On the other hand, a group that emphasizes accountability and in-depth discipleship may need to meet for two hours every week just to give everyone enough time to talk about their faith-lives and spend time in the Bible and prayer.

Meeting Frequency

The more frequently a group meets, the shorter its meetings will probably need to be. Groups that meet weekly often find one-hour meetings sufficient, but groups that meet monthly may need two hours or more.

Balance between Accessibility and Depth

Shorter meetings often attract more people, since

busy people are more willing to commit to that amount of time. The shorter the meeting, however, the more difficult it is to achieve in-depth relationships and sharing. Your meeting length will need to balance those two factors.

Group Members' Life Situations

Some groups keep meeting length short because of child care constraints. Others groups prefer a longer meeting because group members' responsibilities prevent them from meeting frequently.

Time of Day

Groups that meet in the evening may have a clear time limit because most members need to get up early for work the next morning. In the same way, groups that meet before work or during lunch will often last an hour or less because members have to get to work, classes, or other activities.

Group Size

The more people there are in the group, the longer it takes for personal sharing, discussions, and prayer requests. As groups grow, they will usually feel a need to lengthen the meeting time. If this happens to your group, make the decision intentionally, not accidentally. Be sure to ask group members if they want to meet longer, instead of just letting it happen and creating possible schedule problems for some members as a result.

Fellowship Time

In addition to the time groups spend in the four group activities, many groups will regularly have an informal fellowship time before or after the meeting. For example, if a group had a 90-minute meeting, scheduled from 7:00-8:30, group members might start arriving as early as 6:30, and they might stay until 9:00 or later. Group members might come early to chat with one another, and they might stay late for refreshments and social conversation.

If your group regularly comes early or stays late

for fellowship time, make sure visitors and new members know about this custom. That way they will schedule their time (and their baby sitters' time) so that they can stay and enjoy the group fellowship.

The meeting lengths described in the rest of this chapter refer to the time groups spend in the four group activities. Fellowship time needs to be figured over and above these meeting lengths.

One-Hour Meetings

Small groups that meet for one hour or less must be very well-organized and have a clear agenda, since group members frequently have a tight schedule. Leaders of such groups may choose to plan activities to fill about 50 minutes, not 60. This allows for a small amount of fellowship or "getting settled" as group members arrive. Another option is to plan 60 minutes of activities but let group members know that there will be time to chat before or after the meeting for those who can come early or stay late. If you choose this option, you will have to make it very clear when the actual meeting is over and those who need to leave may do so.

What Kinds of Groups Might Meet for One Hour?

There are several kinds of small groups whose membership and missional service activities lend themselves especially well to this short meeting time:

- Breakfast and early-morning groups
- Lunch groups
- Prayer groups
- Sunday morning groups
- Evangelistic groups (that want to keep meetings short so that visitors aren't discouraged by a longer time commitment)

A schedule for an hour-long meeting for a group with six members might look like this:

A Typical One-Hour Meeting Schedule

❑ 1. Check-in and prayer requests (at four minutes
per person) . . . . .24 minutes

❑ 2. Biblical Equipping . . . . .20 minutes

❑ 3. Prayer and worship . . . . .10 minutes

Total . . . . .54 minutes

You may need to explain to group members that such a tight schedule doesn't allow much room for interruptions or variations. If the group agrees to this meeting length, they need to know ahead of time that they may feel rushed at times.

What about such groups' missional service? If they are open groups that actively include visitors and new members, they are being missional by evangelizing. If they are closed groups, they may need to find other times to meet and carry out service to others, or they may periodically devote a whole meeting to service instead of the other activities listed above.

Tips for Short Group Meetings

Short group meetings—an hour or less—may benefit from the following tips.

Encourage group members to stay in contact between meetings to deepen relationships, since you won't have much time for community building.

Vary the focus of your meetings—one week have a longer time for Biblical Equipping, and the next week a longer prayer time.

Ask members to note prayer requests and commit to praying for one another between meetings, rather than taking more time to pray for each request at the group meeting.

Keep your group on the small side—six or seven members rather than nine or ten. This will allow more time for personal sharing and relationship building. You can keep your group at this size either by closing the group (if the group's mission allows this), or by growing to eight members and then dividing the group to form two new groups.

Consider meeting once a week in order to increase the total amount of meeting time.

90-Minute Meetings

90 minutes is the most common length of time for small group meetings. This is long enough for the four group activities, but is short enough for people to feel comfortable coming early or staying late for informal fellowship.

What Kinds of Groups Might Meet for 90 Minutes?

Most groups will probably plan 90 minute meetings, unless they have a good reason to make their meetings shorter or longer.

Tips for 90-Minute Meetings

Even though 90 minutes may seem like plenty of time it can go quickly, especially if you have eight or more group members. The following tips can help you get the most out of your 90-minute meetings.

Get started on time and keep on schedule. Even 90 minutes can feel rushed if you don't use the time well.

Stress different activities at different meetings. Spend extra time on one activity, such as worship, during one meeting or a series of meetings. Then balance that by emphasizing another activity at a series of meetings.

A 90-minute meeting does not require a formal break, but make sure group members know they may get up and attend to their own needs, as necessary.

Be prepared to set aside your agenda if a group member needs the group's immediate attention and care.

The larger your group gets, the more rushed you will feel. This can be a sign that it's time for your group to begin the birthing process and divide into two new groups.[1]

Two-Hour or Longer Meetings

Some small groups regularly meet two hours or more—even some groups that meet every week. (Remember, this means two or more hours spent on the four group activities—fellowship time before or after the meeting is additional.) There are groups that choose to spend two hours a week together in order to make time for all they want to do together. For other groups the meetings last this long because group members get so involved in sharing, praying, and Biblical Equipping that the time just flies by.

If your group meets for two hours or more, make sure you are doing so intentionally, and that group members have agreed to such long meetings. If meetings get longer and longer over time, discuss it with group members and see what they want to do. They may see value in long meetings and decide to continue. They may also prefer to find ways to keep meetings focused and shorter.

What Kinds of Groups Might Meet for Two Hours or More?

Certain kinds of groups can have very good reasons for long meetings.

Groups that meet once a month. If your group only meets once a month, you may need very long meetings to make any progress with community building.

Social groups. Some congregations have small groups that meet once a month at a member's

---

[1] In the ChristCare Series *birthing* does not mean that the "parent" group continues, while a new "child" group begins. Rather, the one group comes to an end and two new groups begin. This acknowledges that both new groups are changing so much that the old group no longer exists, and helps group members grieve the loss of the old group so they will be ready to fully participate in a new group. The ChristCare Series provides thorough training for leading groups through the process of birthing new groups. This training includes a module on bringing closure to groups that are ending, as well as one called Birthing New ChristCare Groups.

home for supper and fellowship. Such meetings are likely to last two or more hours.

Accountability-emphasis groups. Groups committed to focusing on in-depth discipleship may need longer meetings to accomplish their mission.

Service-emphasis groups. A group's service project may take up to a couple of hours. Then, in order to have any time for community building, prayer, or Biblical Equipping, the group may even need to further lengthen the meeting time.

Groups that are meeting less often than normal. For example, groups that meet only once a month during the summer may want to lengthen those meetings, but shorten them again once they go back to their regular schedule.

Tips for Long Meetings

Two or more hours is a long time to sit in one place. Give group members a break during the meeting.

Make sure your meetings really do require this much time. People will resent it if they spend so much of their time only to think it was wasted.

CHAPTER 13

Beginning and Ending on Time

The Importance of Starting and Ending on Time

Regardless of how long you meet, it is extremely important to begin and end group meetings on time. Small group leaders need to respect the commitment that group members make to attend meetings by sticking to agreed upon start and end times. Meetings that start late and end show disrespect for members and often put them in difficult situations.

For example, people who have hired baby-sitters face a difficult choice when a meeting runs late: Do they break their promises about when they said they'd be home, or do they risk embarrassment by leaving the meeting early? Those who have to get up very early for work may have to choose between leaving early or feeling more and more frustrated as the meeting runs late, knowing they'll pay the price in the morning. When people face these problems often, they are more likely to drop out of the group.

There's another problem. When people realize that the group meetings usually start late, many group members start arriving late on a regular basis, thinking, "Oh, I've got time yet." This pattern escalates, and the group meetings start later and later.

Tips for Starting and Ending on Time

As group leader, you are responsible to arrive early. Otherwise you won't be ready to begin the meeting on time.

Wear a watch or have a clock in view to make sure you stay on schedule. You may even want to take your watch off and lay it on a table in front of you so you can check it without being too obvious and distracting others.

Begin on time, regardless of who has (or has not) arrived. When latecomers arrive, welcome them and briefly let them know where you are in the agenda. Starting without them won't offend most people; on the contrary, it lets them know they can count on meetings starting on time.

Plan your meeting agenda carefully so you know how much time you have for each item.

Be ready to set aside your agenda for important matters. If someone is dealing with a crisis, take time to care and support that person. If an especially meaningful discussion is underway, ask the group if they'd like to continue it and then shorten the time allowed for the next item on the agenda.

If an important discussion is taking place at the end of your meeting, say, "It's time for us to end our meeting. If some of you would like to stay, we'll take a short break and continue talking a bit. Those of you who need to leave, feel free to do so." You could also suggest that the discussion carry on into the refreshment time, or that the group pick up the discussion at the next meeting. Be sure, however, not to inconvenience your host by staying too late. If this happens regularly, you may need to re-arrange your meeting schedule so that such discussions (which often grow out of Biblical Equipping time) take place much earlier in the meeting.

Keep refreshments simple and easy to prepare. Then you won't have to deal with group members leaving the meeting early to go into the kitchen to prepare food or drink.

CHAPTER 14

Dealing with Schedule or Location Changes

There will be probably be some times in your group's life when schedule or location changes will be necessary.

Good Reasons to Cancel or Reschedule Meetings

Holidays

Holiday times can get very busy and group members often leave town, so it may make sense to cancel one or two meetings. Try to keep missed meetings to a minimum, though, perhaps with a two-week break at Christmas and one week at Easter.

Summer

Don't stop meeting altogether during the summer, or your group will find it very difficult to get back together in the fall. Group members' need for the group doesn't decrease during the summer, and your group's mission probably doesn't take a vacation for the entire summer. If possible, continue your regular meeting schedule.

If you must plan a reduced summer schedule, consider reducing the number of meetings during times when many group members will be on vacation. However, if it's only one or two members who must be absent, go ahead and meet with the rest of the group.

No One Can Attend

Personal schedules will occasionally get in the way of a group meeting and keep everyone or almost everyone from attending. If only two or three group members will be able to attend on a particular date, you may want to reschedule that group meeting. If this happens frequently, see if your group needs to find a different time to meet.

Seasonal or Work-Related Breaks

Certain community events may necessitate changing your group meeting schedule. Examples include: harvest time in a rural area, activities on a military base, or holidays in a resort town.

Natural Disasters and Other Emergencies

Nature may disrupt your small group meeting schedule with blizzards, thunderstorms, or disasters such as hurricanes or earthquakes.

Unavoidable Meeting Location Changes

Meeting rooms or host homes may become unavailable and force a change. If you cannot find a substitute meeting place, you may need to postpone the meeting.

Guidelines for Making Changes

Since a few schedule changes are inevitable, following are some guidelines to help you deal with them.

Plan Ahead in Order to Avoid Change

Select your meeting place and time wisely and you won't have to change it often. Choose a meeting room that is regularly available to you, reliable hosts, and a meeting time that fits all group members' schedules.

Take into Account the Needs of Group Members without Local Families

Be aware that some group members without family nearby may rely on the group to be their "family" on holidays. If that's the case, either hold group meetings even during the holidays, or else invite those members to join your own family for the holiday. Certainly other group members may also open their homes to those without family in the area.

Make as Few Changes as Possible

Help people get into and stay in the habit of coming to group meetings by making as few changes as possible.

Reschedule Rather Than Cancel

Honor the group members' commitment to the group and express your own by not canceling a meeting unless it is unavoidable. Reschedule meetings if at all possible.

Make Sure Everyone Learns of the Change

Personal phone calls are the best way to make sure group members learn about a change in the meeting place or time. If you leave a message on an answering machine or with someone who answers the phone, ask the person to call you back to confirm that he or she received the message. Otherwise you may want to call back later to double check.

Have a Communication Plan in Place

Group leaders need to set up an emergency communication plan to let group members know when group meetings have been changed. Your plan might be to:

- designate one person for group members to call to find out if the meeting is on or off;

- instruct group members to call your home to find out if the meeting will take place and record a message on your telephone answering machine;

- set up a phone tree;

- choose one group member to contact everyone else in the group, or;

- leave information with the church office and instruct group members to call the church to find out if group meetings have been canceled. (Be sure you check with church staff before choosing this option.)

PART THREE

Creating a Covenant

A small group covenant is the tool group members use to define what they want their relationship with one another to be like. In creating a covenant, group members work together to answer important questions. The covenant is a brief written record of their answers.

Part Three describes what a covenant is and how your group can go about creating one.[1]

---

[1] ChristCare Groups use the course, *Beginnings: A ChristCare Group Experience*, to help build their covenant. The *Beginnings* course contains a sample covenant and tells how to lead group members in deciding what promises their covenant will contain.

CHAPTER 15

Explaining the Value of a Covenant to Your Group

The Necessity of a Covenant

It is impossible for group members to work together effectively without some rules. Every group operates under a "contract," whether it is written down, talked about, or simply understood. When group members create a covenant, however, they intentionally decide what the rules will be, rather than having unspoken rules with which each group member may not fully agree.

Take time to explain the concept of covenant to your small group. Ask them how they feel about creating a covenant. This concept may be new to many group members. Give them time to understand and get used to it. (If they're hesitant, explain that you'd like them to try working under a covenant for a period of time, after which the group can discuss their thoughts and feelings about it.) You can use the following list of benefits to help group members see the value of creating a covenant.

The Benefits of a Covenant

The covenant is the "glue" that keeps the group together and keeps members committed when they feel like giving up. Without a covenant, one or two strong group members may take over and impose their desires on the whole group. If this happened it would cause resentment on the part of less aggressive members, and, if left unchecked, could ultimately destroy the group.

The covenant encourages group members to care for

one another by establishing standards of care and challenging group members to live up to those standards. For example, the covenant should include a promise about confidentiality and another one about showing nonjudgmental, accepting love to one another.

The group leader's effectiveness is sharply reduced without a covenant. It is difficult to hold group members to standards of attendance, confidentiality, and the like if those standards are never spelled out.

A covenant gives group members a tool for holding one another accountable. If all have agreed that attendance is important, and then one member misses several meetings without good reasons, other group members can justifiably express concern and hold the person accountable.

A covenant helps new members become part of the group. The covenant helps new group members understand the group's standards and principles so that they can decide whether they want to join this kind of group.

A covenant can also guide group decisions. In the covenant group members decide what the group's purpose will be. Then they can decide what they will do together in order to carry out the purpose they chose.

CHAPTER 16

Deciding What to Include in Your Covenant

There are three main areas you'll want to focus on when you create your group covenant.

1. Your Group's Mission

In the first part of your covenant your group needs to answer questions such as:

- What is our mission?
- What is our vision for ministry?
- How do we plan to carry out our mission?
- What kind of group will we be? What emphasis, if any, will our group have?

2. Promises Group Members Make to One Another

In order for group members to work together and trust one another, they need to make some important promises described below. As a leader, you can't impose any of these promises on the group; covenants don't work that way. If group members are unwilling to make these promises, however, you will have a very difficult time creating a lasting, Christian small group. Fortunately, most groups readily see the value of these promises.

Confidentiality

Chapter 18 explains the importance of confidentiality in your group. This is a key issue for your covenant.

Relating to One Another Nonjudgmentally

Small group members need to agree to relate to one another with forgiveness and compassion, not with judgment. If group members criticize and judge one another, no one will be willing to share honestly about his or her needs and challenges. Groups must agree to do as Ephesians says: "Put away from you all bitterness and wrath and anger and wrangling and slander, together with all malice, and be kind to one another, tenderhearted, forgiving one another, as God in Christ has forgiven you. Therefore be imitators of God, as beloved children, and live in love, as Christ loved us and gave himself up for us, a fragrant offering and sacrifice to God." (Ephesians 4:31-5:2)

Attendance

You can't have a group if members don't attend meetings. People who regularly miss meetings miss out on the benefits they would have received if they had come, and deprive the group of their personal contributions to the meeting. They also make it neces-sary for the group to take time to bring them up to date at the next group meeting.

Of course, there are some times when group members have no choice but to miss meetings, and this should be acknowledged. In the covenant, how-ever, they promise to attend group meetings whenever possible.

Christian Focus

Occasionally a small group may begin to turn into a mere social club with little or no Christian empha-sis. A small group that wants to maintain its Christian emphasis will want to include that promise in the group covenant.

Visitors and New Members

Will your group be open or closed? Decide that issue and then include your decision in your cov-enant.

3. Decisions about Group Meetings

Your group covenant needs to clearly spell out details about your meetings. Those details include:

- meeting frequency;

- meeting place;
- meeting time;
- refreshments;
- child care;
- recovenanting—that is, how often group members will evaluate the group's life together, and make any necessary changes in the covenant; and
- whether or not smoking will be allowed at group meetings.

CHAPTER 17

When to Recovenant

Each covenant is as unique as the group that writes it. Keep in mind that your covenant is a starting place. You can always revise the covenant as your group members' needs or situations change.

Reasons to Review Your Covenant

A covenant must remain current in order to remain useful. A covenant agreed to many years ago by only a few of the current group members will not fulfill its purpose. There are several reasons why.

Group Members Change

As group members grow spiritually and personally, their interests and needs change also. This means that the group must adjust if it wants to keep meeting members' needs. Recovenanting gives group members the chance to evaluate where the group has been and where they want it to go. It also gives individual group members an opportunity to decide whether they want to continue with the group, or move on.

The Group's Membership Changes

When a group adds members, it changes. The group's covenant may also need to change to reflect new members' needs and concerns. Recovenanting gives new members a chance to contribute to the covenant, modify it, and make it their own.

The Group Loses Missional Focus

Missional service can fall by the wayside if group members don't intentionally commit to it. Regular recovenanting gives group members the chance to evaluate the missional service they have been performing. Then they may decide to continue their missional service, refine it, or do something completely different if God seems to be calling them in a new direction.

Renewed Commitment

Group members' commitment may fade over time if covenant promises are not regularly discussed and affirmed. Recovenanting helps each member remain conscious of commitments, which makes it more likely that those commitments will result in actions. It also allows each member the chance to renew, change, or end his or her own commitment as changed life circumstances or personal growth may dictate.

CHAPTER 18

Explaining the Importance of Confidentiality

It's important for a small group covenant to address the issue of confidentiality. One of your most important jobs as a group leader is to help group members understand and abide by confidentiality.[1]

What Does Confidentiality Mean to Small Groups?

Very simply, confidentiality means that group members promise not to pass on personal, private information, whether it is shared during or between group meetings, without the permission of the person who shared the information.

Why is Confidentiality Important?

Confidentiality is important in small groups because it makes honest and open sharing possible. Before group members can talk about personal concerns, they must be able to trust the group enough to know that the information will not be repeated to others.

What Needs to Remain Confidential?

There are several rules to help you determine what kind of information needs to remain confidential.

Information the Person Has Asked the Group to Keep Confidential

No matter what type of information a group member shares, it must remain confidential if the group member requests it.

---

[1] The ChristCare Group Leader training module, Confidentiality in ChristCare Groups, thoroughly explains how confidentiality works in small groups, and helps small group leaders know how to help group members understand and abide by confidentiality.

Potentially Harmful Information

Information that could harm the group member or others must be kept confidential. For instance, if a group member shares information about his or her upbringing that could cause grief to another family member, the information must be kept confidential.

Public versus Private Information

Anything that a person has probably not revealed outside the group must be kept confidential, no matter how harmless it may seem. The group must assume that information is private unless the person sharing it says he or she won't mind if others outside the group know about it.

When someone shares public information with the group—that is, something that he or she feels good about and won't mind if many others know about—you may consider discussing it elsewhere if you have good reason to do so. For example, if a group member's spouse is in the hospital and you know that there were public prayers for the spouse in the Sunday worship service, you can then tell others about the hospitalization without breaking confidentiality. However, if the group member shares his or her fears about the prognosis during the group meeting, but as far as you know hasn't told anyone else about these fears, that particular information is private and must remain confidential.

If You're Not Sure...

If you're not sure if information is confidential, keep it to yourself until you ask the person who shared it whether or not you may tell anyone else.

A Fence around Confidentiality

Confidentiality is so important that groups need to "build a fence" around it to protect it. Building a fence means taking extra steps to make sure you don't even get close to breaking confidentiality.

This means that before you share public information that the person wouldn't mind having shared, you need to ask yourself if there is a good reason to share the information. Will sharing it help the person or others? If you can't think of a good reason to share the information, keep it to yourself. To repeat: if sharing information doesn't benefit others, don't share it.

If Someone Asks You about Confidential Information

What should you do if someone asks you about something you heard about in your small group meeting? If someone asks you about a specific person or issue, you need to decide if the information is public or private. If it's clearly public, you may consider talking about it, if there's good reason to do so. If it's private or you're not sure, simply say, "I suggest you talk to (the person being discussed) about that." If the other person continues to press you and won't accept that answer, say, "I'm sorry, but our small group has an agreement to keep discussions at our meetings private."

When to Break Confidentiality

There are times when concern for the well-being of another person forces a break in confidentiality.

If you have reason to believe that someone is in danger of committing suicide, or abusing or killing another person, by all means *do not keep silent.* Human life is more precious than the principle of confidentiality. If you learn of a threat of murder or suicide, alert the police, your pastor, and possibly other authorities. It is your Christian responsibility to tell appropriate authorities about suicide, abuse, or threat of murder. This is the most caring act possible for all involved.

CHAPTER 19

Telling Guests and New Members about the Covenant

When your group welcomes guests or new members, the newcomers need to learn about the group's covenant. This protects group members from covenant breaches, and helps guests decide whether or not they want to be part of your group. As group leader you are responsible for ensuring that guests and new members learn about the covenant.

Explain the Covenant to Guests

It is not necessary to tell guests about every aspect of the covenant the first time they visit. For instance, they don't necessarily need to know about child care or refreshments. It *is* necessary, however, for everyone who participates in group meetings to know about two core elements of the covenant: confidentiality and relating to group members in accepting, nonjudgmental ways. Visitors may create embarrassing or painful situations if they don't know about these agreements.

While telling guests about the covenant, you can also remind the rest of the group about the importance of confidentiality and nonjudgmental relating. Take a few minutes at the beginning of the group meeting to welcome the guest and say something like, "We have a couple of rules we consider very important in our group meetings. One is that everything that is said here stays here. We have agreed to keep what goes on at our meetings confidential. The other rule is that we are accepting and nonjudgmental at our meetings. People here have the right to share what they want, as long as it doesn't hurt someone else. We want

our group to be a safe place to share, so we don't criticize one another here."

Explaining the Covenant to New Members

Before a guest becomes a member, he or she
needs to understand and agree to the covenant. So
when someone is interested in joining or has been
coming to group meetings regularly enough to be con-
sidered a member, take the person aside and share the
entire covenant with him or her. Explain that the other
group members have agreed to the covenant, and the
new person now has the opportunity to do so too.

What if a New Member Can't Agree to the Covenant?

What if a new group member has objections to
part of the covenant? If it's something minor that
doesn't greatly affect the rest of the group, the group
might decide that this is not a problem. Suppose, for
example, that the group has covenanted to be on time
for meetings, and the new member must always be 15
minutes late because of a job conflict. The group might
decide to live with the inconvenience, or change the
meeting starting time. However, you should always con-
sult the rest of the group before indicating to the new
member that it's okay to bend a particular group rule.

If a new member's objection cuts to the heart of
the group's life together—for example, if a new member refuses to maintain confidentiality or objects to
the group's Christian nature—then the group leader
needs to talk in-depth with the person and make it
clear that these parts of the covenant so closely define
the nature and purpose of the group that they can't be
changed. People who can't accept them can't join the
group without destroying it. Fortunately, such situations are rare. Very few people who have fundamental
disagreements with a small group's covenant ever
enjoy attending the group enough to want to become
members.

PART FOUR

Housekeeping: Attending to Important Details

Leading a small group means dealing with many essential details. You may have prepared the best Biblical Equipping session ever, but if child care concerns aren't handled well, no one will be able to pay attention to the Biblical Equipping. In the same way, while refreshments may seem like a simple concern, if they aren't handled well they can disrupt the group. Even something as mundane as record keeping can help you be a more caring group leader.

Part Four identifies some of the essential details of group leadership and offers guidelines for handling them effectively.

CHAPTER 20

Working with Meeting Hosts

The duties of a host are simple—to hold the group meeting in his or her home and to make members and guests feel welcome. Hosts may or may not take responsibility for refreshments. Sometimes the host provides beverages, and someone else brings other refreshments.

Members who host group meetings should be willing and eager to do so. Hospitality is not a gift everyone has, so never try to force people to host if they aren't interested.

Sometimes, however, even willing hosts discover that hosting is more of a burden than they can handle. Check periodically to make sure hosts are still willing to do this service. Be especially sure to ask whenever the host's family has new circumstances, such as a new baby, home construction, or a seriously ill family member.

What Hosting Options Are There?

Small groups that meet in members' homes have two hosting options available.

The One-Host Option

There may be one person or couple in your group willing and able to host every meeting. Group members with the gift of hospitality and a home with a room large enough for the group to meet may enjoy doing this. It can become their special ministry.

Your group can make the burden lighter for such a host by helping with any necessary setup before, or cleanup after, the meeting. If your group has refreshments, consider rotating that responsibility so that the host doesn't have to deal with that also. If the host prefers to provide refreshments at each meeting, have a coffee kitty or an offering basket to help defray the costs.

The Several-Hosts Option

If you have several group members willing to serve as hosts, the load will be lighter for each of them. Develop a schedule that evenly spreads the responsibility so that no one gets overburdened with hosting.

It's Okay Not to Host

Probably you will have some group members who are unable or unwilling to host a meeting. Their reasons could involve anything from a small home to discomfort with the role of hospitality provider. If a group member doesn't offer to host, or says "no" when asked directly, accept the decision without questioning it. There is no need to embarrass the member by asking why. Never try to pressure a group member into hosting.

To make it clear to group members that not hosting is okay, you can say something like, "There is no pressure to host. If you don't want to for any reason, just say so. Everyone will respect your decision, and no one will even ask you why." Then keep your word.

Some group members who prefer not to host may agree to take on other responsibilities, such as bringing refreshments or making sure books and supplies make it to the meeting. This can become their form of service. Never imply, however, that members must do such tasks in order to make up for not hosting.

The Group Leader's Responsibility in Hosting

Ultimately, it's the group leader's responsibility to find a meeting place. Having a host doesn't let you off the hook. This means that if your host cancels at the last minute, you must do what you can to find a new location and communicate the change to other group members. (You certainly can ask other group members to help you with these tasks.) If there is no other possible location, you are still responsible for making sure group members know about the cancellation.

The group leader should work with the host to make sure that the group's meeting room is ready. Several concerns you need to consider are listed below.

Checklist for the Host's Home

❑ Make sure the group meeting room is sufficiently private.

❑ Make sure lighting is adequate so everyone can see to read.

❑ Check the room temperature and ventilation and ask the host to adjust it, if necessary. (Note that a room that is cool enough with two people in it may quickly become too warm with ten people in it.)

❑ Arrange comfortable chairs in a circle so everyone can see and hear one another.

❑ Have a plan to deal with phone calls or family visitors who come to the door.

❑ Ask if there are any special household arrangements the group should know about—for example, using the upstairs bathroom because the downstairs bathroom is being repaired.

As people become accustomed to hosting group meetings, they will cover the details on the list by themselves. You won't need to review the list with the host every time. If problems crop up, you can always refer back to the list.

CHAPTER 21

Taking Care of Child Care

If your group includes parents of young children, you will need to consider child care arrangements. You can't afford to ignore this issue—it's often one of the main reasons that group members are absent or drop out, or simply never join your group in the first place.

Group members without young children may not realize just how difficult it is for parents to find appropriate child care, so you may need to help them understand the parents' situation. Groups can show Jesus' care to parents by helping them handle their need for appropriate child care. This helps parents meet their primary responsibility to their children and still participate as valued group members. Following are some suggestions.

Guidelines to Consider for Child Care

Take the following guidelines into account as you work on child care.

Choose child care that:

Is safe. Above all, be sure the children are safe with the caregivers you choose. Carefully choose baby-sitters who will protect the children and watch them carefully. This is a critical issue in a time when abuse is becoming more prevalent, even in churches. Also be sure that the child care environment is clean and free from safety hazards. Unless you have young children or grandchildren, you may not notice all the items in a room that could harm children. In such a case you may even want to ask the parents of young children to check out the area and make sure there are no safety hazards.

Benefits the children. The best choice for children is one they can enjoy and learn from.

Is workable for all the parents. Find a solution that works for all the group members, not just some of them.

Is affordable. Be sensitive to group members who can't afford to pay much, even if they hesitate to admit that to the group. Be sure you have everyone's input before making a decision that requires group members to pay.

Is reliable. You need a plan you can put in place and then count on—not one that requires tinkering and adjusting every week.

Is nondisruptive. Find a form of child care that disrupts the group meeting as little as possible.

What Are the Options?

There are several child care possibilities available to small groups.

Children Present at Meetings

In most cases, this doesn't work. Adults get distracted, and children get bored. The only exceptions to this rule would be very young infants (likely to sleep through the meeting, or in need of nursing) or a special intergenerational small group (with limited expectations regarding benefits for adult members). Try to find a better solution.

Parents Arrange Their Own Child Care

This works well if all of the parents have little trouble finding and paying for child care. It also allows parents to attend evening group meetings without worrying about getting home by their children's bedtime. With this option, the group doesn't need to get involved in providing child care.

If your group seems to be moving in this direction, make sure everyone has a chance to speak and share any concerns about this decision. Some parents have real difficulties finding or affording child care, but may hesitate to say so if they believe they're the only ones in the group who have a problem in this area. They may fear becoming a burden to the group or feeling "different" from everyone else. Be sure your group doesn't make a quick decision that leaves these members without the child care they need, or that stretches their budget farther than they can afford.

Group Members Take Turns Providing Child Care

Some groups try to save money by having parents take turns as baby-sitters. Avoid this if at all possible. Parents who miss meetings to serve as baby-sitters disrupt the group's continuity and growth as a Christian community. Someone is always absent, and someone else needs to be filled in on what happened at the last meeting. It's much better to have all members present and hire a sitter. Also remember that some parents come to group meetings partly as a "vacation" from the demands of caring for their children's minute-to-minute needs. While they love their children, they also feel the need for adult companionship, and the group meeting provides this. Having parents take turns baby-sitting undermines this benefit.

Several Families Share Child Care

If there are several families with young children in the group, consider arranging joint child care. Several parents might arrange for a sitter to watch their children at one home. This has three advantages. First, it's usually easier to find one sitter than to find two or three. Second, since the children are at another location, the group meeting isn't disrupted. Third, a child's home is usually much more comfortable for the children themselves. It is more likely to be safe and to contain interesting toys and comfortable play areas.

If you choose this solution, one parent needs to be responsible for getting the baby-sitter and providing the home. It's best if the home is near the group meeting site, so parents can be just a few minutes away from their children. Also, depending on the number and ages of the children, group members may need two or more sitters to provide adequate care.

One disadvantage to this setup is that several sets of parents are left scrambling for alternate arrangements if either the sitter or the home becomes unavailable at the last minute. Have a backup plan for such emergencies. For example, you might decide that parents will bring children to the meeting and the group will just make do for that one meeting.

Providing Child Care at the Meeting Site

Some groups choose to hire one or two sitters to care for children at the meeting location, a choice that has several advantages. It eliminates travel time to a sitter or another home and assures parents of regular, reliable child care. In addition, parents are able to reach their children quickly in case of emergency.

Unfortunately, this solution also makes it much easier for children to disrupt a group meeting. If you choose this option, find a room for the children as far away from the group meeting as possible. Make sure the sitter knows that children are not allowed to interrupt parents unless absolutely necessary.

If the meeting takes place in a home, prepare well. Make sure the child care room is child-proof. Move delicate vases and fascinating trinkets. Think about bathrooms, refrigerators, and microwave ovens for heating bottles—will the baby-sitter or the children have to walk through the group meeting in order to reach them? Consider activities for the children—are there crayons, paper, or toys that children may use? Will parents bring these from home?

If the meeting and child care take place at church, try to put the children in a nursery, playroom, or other area where there are plenty of toys and few dangers. Clear your use of the room with the appropriate church authorities and get a key. Make sure bathrooms are unlocked and refrigerators are available (if necessary).

Others in the Congregation Provide Child Care

In some congregations there may be people who support small group ministry by caring for children whose parents are at group meetings. This might even be a missional service project of another small group. In such a case, they might provide child care in a home or at the church building.

Providing Supplies

Whatever child care arrangements your group makes, members will need to make sure supplies are available for the children.

Child Care Supplies

- books, toys, and games;
- a first-aid kit;
- refreshments (even something as simple as crackers and juice);
- extra diapers and related paraphernalia;
- paper towels for inevitable spills and accidents;
- an emergency phone number for the sitter to use if the group meeting is held elsewhere. Be sure that the sitter has easy access to a phone (and all other materials) without needing to leave the children unattended.

Guidelines for Handling Sick or Misbehaving Children

Sick Children

Make sure group members agree not to bring sick children. While this might seem like common sense, don't count on everyone thinking of it. Spell out what you mean by sickness: a fever, cough, vomiting, sore throat, or a rash that isn't completely gone 24 hours before the meeting. (Grade schools and pre-schools usually have similar guidelines.) Make sure parents know that caring for a sick child is an acceptable excuse for missing the group meeting. Of course, if a child becomes sick during a meeting, the sitter should let the parent know right away.

Misbehaving Children

It's a little more difficult to know what to do in

the case of children who act up, misbehave, or hurt other children. Sitters can handle most problems that occur. But if there is a serious problem, the sitter needs to know to call a parent. In some cases that may be all that's required. But children who are often uncontrollable, or who regularly behave in ways that hurt themselves or others, may have to stop participating in the child care group.

In such a situation, involve the parent and the sitter in the decision. (Keep it private. This doesn't need to be a whole-group discussion unless the behavior has affected most or all of the group.) Explain the reasons for it. Parents may be understanding, embarrassed, or possibly angry at the decision. Listen, but don't compromise on what you know is best.

Avoiding Potential Child Abuse

Unfortunately, child abuse is an issue even in Christian churches, and one you can't afford to ignore. Carefully check the references of anyone who provides care to your group's children. (Some churches run a police records check.) If it's financially possible, have at least two sitters present at all times. Instruct sitters to leave the door ajar when they take young children to the bathroom, or to have another sitter accompany them. This is for the sitter's legal protection as much as for the child's sake.

It's wise to have the child care take place in a relatively public place—say, in a room with an open door (and a child safety gate) situated right next to the bathroom. Then parents on the way to and from the rest room will have the opportunity to look in and see what's going on. If this isn't possible, arrange for unannounced "drop by" visitors—perhaps the host of the group meeting. (If small children are likely to be upset if they see their parents before it's time to go home, have another group member look in.) It may disrupt the group meeting a bit to have someone step out for a moment to do this, but it's well worth the added safety.

Pay attention to anything that seems odd—closed doors or strange "games" that children talk about later. Immediately follow up on such reports. Being aware of the possibility of child abuse is the first step toward making sure it never happens to the children cared for during your small group meetings.

Including Children in a Group Meeting

It's wise to include children in your group meeting once or twice a year. It can help them understand what their parents are doing, and it may also help them grow as young Christians. Getting to know one another's families also aids community building. Here are some suggestions:

Bible Story Night

Ask each family to prepare a Bible story to act out during the group meeting. You might also work in crafts and other vacation church school activities.

Group Picnic or Outing

Schedule an outing or activity that everyone—adults and children—will enjoy.

Different Meetings for Children of Different Ages

Invite children of different ages—preschoolers, grade-schoolers, teenagers—to different meetings. Plan each meeting to be meaningful to the children present.

CHAPTER 22

Planning for Refreshments

Small group meetings often include refreshments. Refreshments can add to members' enjoyment, and help create a relaxed setting for community building.

When to Serve Refreshments

At the Beginning of the Meeting

Serving beverages at the beginning of the meeting can be a great way to help people get comfortable. Holding a cup gives people something to do with their hands during the sometimes awkward moments at the start of the meeting, especially if they don't yet know many people. Talking about refreshments also facilitates interaction between group members who don't know one another very well.

During the Break?

If you have a longer meeting—two hours or more—it is wise to have a break in the middle. While this seems to be a logical time to serve refreshments, be aware of some possible problems.

First, it's especially important to have simple and quick refreshments if they are served in the middle of a meeting. If the refreshments are too time-consuming, you can lose valuable time needed for the second half of your meeting.

Second, refreshments signal a time to relax. If you need group members' full attention in the second half of the meeting, that may be difficult to get once they have shifted into a relaxed and socializing mode.

Third, refreshments that require immediate cleanup can consume a lot of time. Choose refreshments that require little cleanup, such as cookies or crackers on paper napkins.

At the End of the Meeting

Probably the best time to serve refreshments is at the end of the meeting. Then people can feel free to relax and socialize. Those who have to leave early will miss only the refreshments instead of part of the meeting. Preparation and cleanup won't take time away from the meeting. Enjoying refreshments can be a pleasant way to end the time together.

Who Should Provide Refreshments?

The easiest solution to providing refreshments is for group members to take turns sharing both the cost and the responsibility. If your group takes turns meeting in each member's home, the host for each meeting might be the best person to provide refreshments.

Some members may be unable or unwilling to provide refreshments. This could be a matter of cost, time, or simple lack of interest. Don't pressure anyone to provide refreshments. If some members choose not to provide them, they may be able to help defray others' costs by contributing to a kitty.

One or two group members may really enjoy providing refreshments and want to make it their ministry to the group. In that case, group members should thankfully receive this ministry and leave the refreshments to the "experts." Offer to share the cost, but don't insist. Check periodically to see if these group members are still willing to continue providing refreshments. Also check to see if anyone else would like to get involved.

When to Omit Refreshments

There are times when you might decide not to include refreshments as part of your group meeting.

When one or more group members are on strict diets. Your group might choose to be sensitive to the dietary needs of a group member by not having refreshments at all. Or group members might agree to bring only those foods that the person may eat, for example, low-fat or sugar-free foods.

When the group decides not to have refreshments. Some groups decide that refreshments are just too much work and are not necessary to the group's effectiveness. If finding group members to provide refreshments is difficult or causes problems among group members, the group can choose not to include refreshments in their meetings.

When the meeting location prohibits food. A meeting location (such as a special room in a church) might have restrictions that prevent a group from bringing food or beverages into the room.

General Guidelines

Some general guidelines for appropriate refreshments are listed below.

Beverages. Most groups provide beverages, even if they do not provide food. Consider having both hot and cold beverages available.

Snack food. Keep food simple. Explain to your group that expensive refreshments aren't necessary, and help members avoid competing to see who can make the best or most elaborate refreshments.

Preparation. Avoid refreshments requiring extensive on-site preparation, since this is likely to take the preparer away from the group early, or force members to stay late as they wait for them to be ready.

CHAPTER 23

Respecting the Host's Home

There are certain standards of behavior that group members must observe when they meet in someone's home. Even though you *hope* group members will all be naturally thoughtful, courteous, and kind, don't assume that this will always be the case. You might want to write down some "rules of etiquette" and give them to every group member. That way everyone knows what to expect. A sample code of conduct is shown below.

Rules of Etiquette for Small Groups

1. Don't arrive too early, and don't leave too late. Your host needs preparation time before the meeting and may have to get up early the next morning.

2. Stay out of rooms you haven't been invited into.

3. If you make a mess, clean it up.

4. Don't tie up your host's phone with personal calls.

5. Prepare refreshments that don't require extensive use of your host's kitchen and appliances.

6. Don't use your host's television or stereo without permission.

7. Don't smoke in your host's home without permission.

There are certainly exceptions to these rules. For example, in an emergency, you may need to make a long-distance personal phone call from your host's phone. If so, ask permission. Use your telephone credit card, if possible, otherwise reimburse your host for the cost. Don't impose on a host by asking to do this again and again.

When Something is Damaged

What if the host's home is damaged or something is broken? As a general rule, if a group member breaks or damages something, he or she should offer to pay for it.

What if the item is so expensive—such as an antique vase—that the group member can't afford to pay for it? In such a case, the group needs to consider all the possibilities. Will the homeowner's insurance pay for all or part of the expense? Do the group members need to pitch in and help pay for the damage? Sometimes the host will graciously choose to absorb the cost.

Groups run the risk of doing damage whenever they meet in someone's home. Inform your hosts about this possibility from the beginning. If it occurs, group members need to work together to do the right thing.

CHAPTER 24

Record Keeping for Your Small Group

As small group leader, you will need to keep some simple group records or see that someone else does.

The Value of Record Keeping

Record keeping is important for several reasons. It enables you to check the facts about your group's activities. This can help you avoid problems such as asking the same person to bring refreshments six times in a row, or never asking one particular group member to lead prayers even though he or she has been waiting for a chance to do so.

Record keeping also gives you a picture of your group through time. As you look back on the attendance records, you may discover that attendance dips every year at a certain time—summer, for instance. Then you can anticipate such trends, perhaps planning a different meeting schedule for that time of year.

Record keeping gives you opportunities to care. When you know that a group member lost a child in a car accident three years ago this Tuesday, you can make a special effort to visit, call, or send a card to say you are thinking of, and praying for, him or her. You can also encourage other group members to express care at such times. Similarly, if you have a list of birthdays and addresses, you (or someone you delegate this responsibility to) can send cards to group members on their special days. It gives your group another chance to say "We care about you." Even your attendance record may give you an opportunity to care, by leading you to find out why a member has been absent.

As you can see, even this mundane task can become a form of missional service. Let your record keeping be your servant, not your master, helping you as you serve God and God's people.

What Records Might You Keep?

The first rule of group record keeping is to do what those who oversee your congregation's small group ministry ask. Your congregation may want certain kinds of information recorded or a special form used. Follow those instructions.

The following lists provide some record keeping suggestions.

Records You May Want to Keep

- A current copy of your meeting schedule (giving dates and locations, if you meet in several homes on a rotating basis)
- A list of group members' names, addresses, and phone numbers for home and work (check to be sure it's okay to call at work)
- A completed copy of your group's covenant
- A list of curriculum materials your group has already used
- A record of when members have hosted (in order to help you rotate this function)
- A record of when group members have brought refreshments
- An attendance record
- A birthday and anniversary calendar
- Reminders of anniversaries of group members' significant losses (such as the death of a loved one), so you can offer special care to those members on that date
- A list of prayer requests, including answers that you know of
- A record of when people have led group

prayers, or Bible studies, or otherwise fulfilled group ministry functions

- A list of visitors to the small group, including their names, addresses, phone numbers, and dates of visits

It's best to keep all these records in one place—perhaps a three-ring notebook into which you can insert new records as needed. Bring this notebook with you to every meeting, so you don't have to rely on memory or scribbled notes when you get home.

You may want to put together an information sheet that each group member fills out in order to gather the information about them that you want to keep.

Sharing Record Keeping Tasks

You might want to delegate record keeping to a reliable group member. If you do this, be sure that the group member knows exactly what information you need and how to record it. Ask the person to give you regular reports on matters such as upcoming birthdays or who is hosting the next meeting. Periodically check with the member to make sure everything's going all right, and to make yourself aware of any important information (such as a dip in attendance) that you might not see otherwise.

You might also decide to share the record keeping responsibilities while keeping for yourself the ones that most directly affect your role as small group leader. For example, you should keep the attendance records when you are the one who calls absent group members. You should also keep the phone number list. The birthday list, on the other hand, should be in the hands of the person who has volunteered to send cards. Another member might agree to keep track of the list of prayer requests and answers.

Make arrangements so that you periodically receive up-to-date copies of the records that others keep. Review all group records yourself on a regular basis, and be sure that you have the records you need for completing any required reports.

Providing Information to Group Members

Some of the records you keep would also be helpful for group members to have. For example, a phone list will help group members keep in touch and also call to request prayers. If every group member has a list of birthdays and anniversaries, some might choose to send special greetings or telephone other members on those days. Just remember to check with all group members to make sure they don't mind before you pass out such records.

Records you might share with group members include a roster of all group members, including names, addresses, and phone numbers; birthdays and anniversaries; a list of upcoming meeting dates and locations and a list of who has refreshment responsibilities for the next several months.

PART FIVE

Leading: Issues of Ongoing Group Life

Once you have attended to all the details of establishing your group, you are freer to experience the joy of participating in ongoing group life. Even then, however, there are still nuts and bolts issues to attend to. Your leadership in these areas will help your group remain enjoyable and missional.

CHAPTER 25

Sharing Leadership Responsibilities

Effective small group leaders don't do all the leading. Instead, they *share* leadership, enabling as many members as possible to serve the whole group and help it run well. Group members may share leadership tasks such as leading the opening prayer, coordinating refreshments, taking responsibility for communication between meetings, or leading the group in Biblical Equipping. Indeed, one way to measure a small group leader's success is by how many group members he or she eventually includes in group leadership.

Why Share Leadership?

There are many good reasons for a small group leader to share leadership.

To Discover Future Leaders

When group members have opportunities to exercise leadership, they may be surprised to find they enjoy it. Sometimes they discover that they would like to develop their leadership skills further. They often eagerly take on additional responsibilities. With experience, and the small group leader's encouragement, some of these group members will eventually become group leaders themselves.

To Identify an Apprentice

Part of your responsibility as a group leader is to identify and work with an apprentice group leader. Sharing leadership is the best way to identify those with the gifts and the inclination to serve as apprentices.[1]

To Acknowledge God's Gifts in Others

Small groups enable members to discover the gifts God has given them and affirm God's gifts in others. Sharing leadership is a good way of encouraging group members to recognize these Spirit-given gifts.

To Share the Burden of Caring

Practically every member will experience life difficulties and need the group's care at some point. Whether a member is hospitalized, recently unemployed, or suffering some other crisis, the whole group needs to respond by supporting, praying, and caring for the member. Shared group leadership helps members realize that this kind of Christian care is not just the group leader's responsibility, but everyone's.

To Lighten the Work Load

Delegating tasks can help lighten the load of leading a small group.

What Leadership Tasks To Share

Some responsibilities that are easy and appropriate to share are listed below.

Tasks to Delegate

- scheduling, preparing, and serving refreshments;
- planning meeting locations and communicating those plans to group members;
- following up with visitors who attend your group;
- leading opening and closing prayers;

---

[1] In the ChristCare Series a group member serves as an apprentice in order to learn what the job of small group leader entails, and to decide whether he or she wants to train as a ChristCare Group Leader. The apprenticeship doesn't provide all of the training necessary to serve as a group leader. Apprentices also participate in ChristCare Group Leader training in order to learn what they need to be effective ChristCare Group Leaders.

- helping care for group members in crisis;
- recognizing special days, such as birthdays and anniversaries;
- keeping records;
- arranging child care; and
- leading Biblical Equipping sessions.

Tasks Not to Delegate

There are also some responsibilities that group leaders should *not* delegate, including:

- supervising the apprentice group leader;
- taking responsibility for securing the group's meeting place;
- acting as a liaison between the group and the congregation's Equippers or small group ministry administrators;
- helping a group member who needs more care than the group can provide receive a referral for additional care, and;
- taking final responsibility for everything needed to make the group work well.

How To Delegate Leadership Tasks

When you delegate a task, you must know enough about it to tell if it is being done correctly. When you understand the task and know how to do it yourself, you can be a good "coach": offering direction, giving advice, providing support, and answering questions.

When you delegate, clearly explain what needs to be done, how to do it, and when it needs to be done. You may even want to write out your instructions ahead of time, to be sure that they're clear and well-organized. Then you can reinforce your verbal instructions to the person by handing him or her the written ones.

When you first give the assignment, let the other person know that you'll check in to see how things are going. You can also tell the person when you want him or her to check in with you. If, at check-in time you find a problem, investigate it. Find out if you need to explain the assignment more clearly, or if the person needs help. Maybe you need to work together to come up with a better plan for accomplishing the task. If you and the person decide that he or she cannot complete the task, assign part or all of it to someone else, or do it yourself.

Once the person has established a positive track record, you won't need to keep such close tabs on him or her. Yet you still need to remember that, as group leader, you have the final responsibility. Your supervision shows that you care about the work and about the person doing it.

CHAPTER 26

Cultivating Consistent Attendance

Is attendance at small group meetings important? Absolutely! Only those who come to group meetings can fully benefit from, and contribute to, the group. Attendance problems can indicate larger problems in the group's dynamics or in members' lives.

Caring about attendance is an important way small group leaders demonstrate Christ's care for group members. You need to help group members understand the value of attendance, respond when people are absent, provide care for group members who are absent because of crises, and sometimes help group members with ongoing problems decide whether or not they will continue in the group.

Why Attendance Matters

There are several important reasons for regular attendance.

Attendance is necessary for the group to fulfill its mission. No matter what the group's mission is—from evangelism to supporting one another in individual ministries—absent members impair the group's ability to serve.

Attending is each group member's responsibility. Being a group member isn't an honorary position, but an active responsibility and privilege. Attendance is essential if the group member is to contribute to the growth of other members and of the group itself.

Attendance is necessary for community building. Small groups build relationships and trust at every meeting. Members get to know one another—and become comfortable sharing personal thoughts and feelings—by spending time together. Irregular attendance can greatly inhibit this atmosphere of trust. When certain group members drop in only occasionally, others don't know them well enough to feel comfortable sharing personal concerns with them. As a result, the whole group may stay on a superficial level.

Attendance is necessary for continuity. When group members are absent, they miss whatever new insights the group gained during study and discussion, and they aren't aware of any new needs for care.

A group isn't a group without members present. Each member has gifts and talents that no one else in the group has. If the group has ten members and one is absent, ten percent of the group is gone. The whole group is at least ten percent poorer in caring, insight, and understanding.

C.S. Lewis would put the percentage of group impoverishment much higher. "Lamb says somewhere that if, of three friends (A, B, and C), A should die, then B loses not only A, but 'A's part in C,' while C loses not only A but 'A's part in B.' In each of my friends there is something that only some other friend can fully bring out. By myself I am not large enough to call the whole man into activity; I want other lights than my own to show all his facets. . . Of course, the scarcity of kindred souls—not to mention practical considerations about the size of rooms and the audibility of voices—set limits to the enlargement of the circle; but within those limits we possess each friend not less but more as the number of those with whom we share him increases."[1] Each group member is a

---

[1] C.S. Lewis, *The Four Loves* (New York: Harcourt Brace & Company, 1988), pages 61-62.

vital and irreplaceable part of the group. The group simply isn't the same when members are missing.

When It's Okay Not to Attend

Naturally, there are times in every group member's life when he or she will not be able to attend a group meeting. To communicate the importance of attendance to your small group, review the following list together. Ask members if they can think of any other times when absence would be acceptable.

Good Reasons for Not Attending

- Emergencies
- Trips out of town
- Personal illness
- Illness of a family member requiring care

Handling Acceptable Absences

Make sure all the members of your group know to tell somebody if they must be absent. In many groups, members call the leader ahead of time. (This is especially important if the leader was expecting the person who must be absent to help lead the meeting.) In other groups, members call the host at the home where the meeting will be held. If group members can't reach the appropriate person, ask them to call other group members until they reach someone who will be attending the meeting. This way, your group won't wonder or worry about an absent member.

When a group member is ill and calls ahead to let you know he or she can't come to a meeting, you can:

- Thank the member for calling and make sure he or she knows when and where the next meeting is.
- Call the member a day or so after the meeting, to give an update on what occurred at the meeting and to see how the person is feeling.
- Encourage other group members to contact the absent member by calling or writing.

When a member responsible for some aspect of the group meeting must be absent, there are a few possible ways of handling it.

- If you have enough advance notice, ask someone else to take over the task.

- If you don't have enough advance notice, you'll have to find some way to fulfill the person's responsibility: skip refreshments or bring them yourself, lead Biblical Equipping or do something else in its place, and so on.

- Be willing to pitch in as needed. As group leader, it's your job to answer the question, "What do we do now?"

When a group member misses a meeting without notifying anyone, be sure to:

- Call the person in order to communicate that you care. You're not "checking up" because he or she has done something wrong. You are calling because you care enough to notice the absence and find out if everything is all right.

- Put some action into your care, when that seems appropriate. If the person is ill, a card or a prepared meal might be appreciated. If there's a crisis, it might be an opportunity for other group members to become involved in caring.

Handling Absences without Good Reasons

When you contact absent group members, you may find out that they did not have good reasons for being absent. Here are some suggestions for handling situations in which a group member missed a group meeting because "I didn't want to miss a show on TV," "We decided to have friends over for dinner," or "I just didn't feel like coming."

A First Occurrence

If this is the first time this has happened with this group member, say that you hope he or she will make group meetings a top priority in the future. Remind the group member of the importance of attending and of the promise to attend faithfully that everyone made in the group covenant.

A Regular Occurrence

If a particular group member is regularly absent for no good reason, find out why. Has the person lost interest in the group? Have his or her personal needs or expectations of the group changed? Has the group grown so large that this person no longer feels needed or included? Did this person have his or her feelings hurt? Is the person going through a difficult time in his or her spiritual life? Talk with the person and listen to find out if there are any hidden reasons for the absences.

Address the Problem, if Possible

After you find out why a group member is often absent, do what you can, if anything, to address the situation. For instance, if your group is so large that members are feeling left out, that is a clear sign that it is time to divide your group into two new groups. If the group member is no longer interested in what the group is doing, you might recommend a small group with a different emphasis—one that better fits the member's needs. If the person is feeling angry or sad about something that happened in the group, work with group members to resolve the situation that caused hurt feelings.

Ask the Group Member to Decide

If the group member truly is interested in the group, but is simply too busy to attend, help the member decide what to do next. The group member might choose to eliminate another activity to make more time for the group. He or she might also decide to leave the group until he or she has more time available. The group member needs to decide what he or she is going to do, because attending infrequently is not a valid choice. It just isn't in the best interest of the whole group and it hinders the group's mission.

Be Caring and Assertive

Do your best to be nonjudgmental when talking with a group member who has an attendance problem, but do be caring and assertive. You give people an opportunity to grow when you hold them accountable for their decisions.

Attendance Expectations for Guests

The attendance expectations your group holds for members do not apply to visitors—even regular visitors who are thinking about joining the group. Until people commit to the covenant, absences are acceptable. Make a caring phone call when a regular visitor misses a group meeting, but go easy on the accountability until the person is ready to make a commitment.

CHAPTER 27

Dealing with Habitual Lateness

Being late for a small group meeting now and then is probably unavoidable. If a group member is habitually late, however, you need to respond.

The Problem with Habitual Lateness

You need to let an habitually late member know how this disruptive behavior harms the group. Latecomers interrupt important activities. The group must stop and wait for latecomers to get settled, and information may have to be repeated. Sometimes the latecomer interrupts a group member who is sharing deeply personal feelings, or the entire group in its time of worship. This can strain the group's sense of community and fragile bond of trust. One member's habitual lateness often discourages others from trying to be prompt, since lateness shows disrespect for others' time. None of this is good for the group.

Habitual lateness also hurts the latecomer. A group member who is habitually late misses out on group activities. He or she may miss group prayer time if that comes early, or else miss check in time and not hear what is happening in the lives of other group members. Whatever activity the latecomer misses, he or she is less a part of the group for not having been there. That diminishes his or her role in supporting the group's mission, as well as in giving and receiving care within the group.

Addressing the Issue of Habitual Lateness

When you realize that a group member has a problem with habitual lateness, try to find out why.

Does the person work later or have a longer commute than others in the group? Is the group member the primary caretaker of an aging parent or of young children who require extra care? Once you know what the reason for the problem is, you'll have a better idea of how to deal with it.

Reasons for Habitual Lateness

There are two general reasons for habitual lateness: unavoidable circumstances or lack of consideration.

Unavoidable Lateness

If a person is habitually late because of work demands, child or parent care issues, or other unavoidable circumstances, encourage group members to demonstrate Christ's care by being sensitive and empathic. Invite the person to explain why he or she is often late. Ask the group to discuss whether they need to change the meeting schedule or location to help the person arrive on time. Lead group members in brainstorming possible solutions.

You may discover that there is no perfect solution to the problem. In that case, the group and the habitually late member need to choose a less satisfactory solution. You may need to help the person find another group that meets at a more convenient time. It may be painful for the group to lose a member this way, but it might be best for all involved.

The group might also choose to live with the interruptions and other disadvantages caused by one member's regular tardiness. In such a case, group members should thoroughly discuss their options and intentionally choose to live with the inconvenience.

Inconsiderate Lateness

If a group member is habitually late because he or she is forgetful—or just doesn't realize how important it is to be on time—there are steps you can take. Begin by talking privately with the person. Emphasize the effect that his or her lateness is having on the group. If this doesn't work, bring up the issue at a meeting and ask group members to express their feelings. Sometimes it takes the whole group to help the always-late member to acknowledge the problem's significance. Note that this group discussion is not a time to attack the habitually late group member. It should be a time to express Christian care and concern by holding the member accountable to the group covenant and emphasizing how the group's mission depends on group members living up to their covenant commitments.

Dealing openly with a problem may seem difficult, but it is actually a healthy sign. It shows that the group cares enough about itself and its members to talk openly about what's going on. You can support this kind of caring accountability by facilitating such a discussion.

CHAPTER 28

Encouraging Members to Complete Assignments

Uncompleted assignments have an effect similar to frequent absences and habitual lateness: group members hurt themselves and the rest of the group. They can't participate fully in the Biblical Equipping session because they haven't prepared. Since group members learn from one another in Biblical Equipping, people who don't prepare hold others back. Make it clear to group members that the group expects them to do reading assignments (if any) and to do their best at Biblical Equipping Apart, the part of Biblical Equipping done between meetings. Group members have a right to expect this of one another.

Responding Appropriately When Assignments Aren't Done

It's important for you to respond when a group member isn't doing assignments. You need to find out why this is happening. What's going on in a person's life that might make completing assignments difficult? Perhaps they've been preoccupied with a personal crisis or with family problems. Are they just forgetful? Maybe there are some unresolved faith or emotional issues that make Bible study uncomfortable. Whatever the reason, discovering it is the first step toward responding to it.

If it's not one or two people but the entire group failing to complete assignments, find out why. Maybe the curriculum or topic is the problem. Perhaps you or your group "bit off more than you could chew." If so, lead the group in choosing a different topic.

Check to see if the pace is too fast, or the reading

assignments are too long. Perhaps each session covers too much information. Try spending two sessions on the material you would normally cover in one.

If your group members are exceptionally busy people, try reducing what you expect of them between meetings. You might also give different reading assignments to different people instead of having everyone do all of them. Then ask each person to share what he or she learned with the whole group during the discussion.

CHAPTER 29

Helping Members with Transportation Needs

There may be times when group members need help getting to and from group meetings.

Occasional Needs for a Ride

When a car is in the shop or there is another temporary problem, group members should feel free to call one another and ask for a ride. Group members care for one another in many ways. Sometimes that means helping out with simple needs, such as a ride to the group meeting.

Ongoing Needs for Transportation Help

Some small groups have members who, because of physical or financial limitations, are never able to provide their own transportation. Help group members demonstrate care for the person by helping with this problem.

Responding to Ongoing Transportation Problems

Group members take turns providing a ride. This solution gives everyone the chance to spend extra time with the person, and no one has all the responsibility. Someone needs to keep track of drivers and make sure they know when it's their turn. Perhaps the person receiving the rides could call and confirm before each meeting.

One group member provides rides. There may be one group member who freely chooses to provide a ride for this member every time. This becomes one of his or her ministries.

Hold group meetings at the home of the person without transportation. Obviously, this solution works only if the member is willing and able to host group meetings.

Help solve related problems. Perhaps the person has a broken-down car and can't afford repairs. You might have one group member who could care for the person by volunteering to fix it for the cost of parts. Or, some members might be able to recommend a mechanic who will fix the car for a reasonable price.

Small group leaders should not try to solve members' transportation difficulties on their own. That deprives other group members of a chance to care. Instead, present this difficulty to the group as an opportunity for group members to care for one another, grow in faith, and follow Jesus' example of servanthood.

When You Feel Manipulated

Some people seem to have more than their share of "emergencies." One or more group members may feel manipulated by someone who always calls at the last minute, never takes responsibility for him- or herself, or never expresses gratitude for help received. In such circumstances encourage members to be assertive and set clear limits on what they are willing and able to offer.

CHAPTER 30

Communicating between Meetings

Group leaders are responsible for communication with group members between meetings. There are several kinds of information that may need to be communicated, by the group leader or by group members, in a variety of ways.

What Needs to Be Communicated?

News or Reminders about Group Meetings

Group members need to learn about any changes in upcoming meetings, such as:

- canceled or rescheduled meetings;
- changes in time or location; or
- changes in the assignments to be completed before the meeting.

Group leaders may also want to remind members about tasks they've agreed to do, such as hosting, bringing refreshments, or leading prayer.

News about Group Members

Let the group know quickly if members have any very good news, such as the birth of a child or being hired for a job after long unemployment. Also communicate any serious bad news, such as an injury or the death of a family member. That way group members can pray for one another, call to offer support, and help in other ways. (Just be sure you get permission before sharing news.)

Assurances of Care

Whenever a group member misses a meeting without letting someone know why, follow up the next day with a phone call. This is not an opportunity to criticize, but rather an expression of care and concern. By calling you will often learn about crises and needs in members' lives. Such calls can also encourage attendance, since group members know they will receive a call after a missed meeting.

If a group member is going through a tough time, find ways to reach out to him or her between meetings. Send cards or notes, offer support, or call to listen and empathize. If a group member experiences a major crisis such as a hospitalization, the group may communicate care by visiting, caring for children, providing transportation, bringing over meals for other family members, or other tangible kinds of care.[1]

Ways to Communicate between Meetings

In-person visits provide support during a difficult time. When a group member experiences a crisis, your presence communicates care and support.

Phone calls act as reminders, requests, follow-ups, or check-ins. One personal phone call reminding a group member about the next meeting is worth at least three postcards and six bulletin announcements. Whenever you make a phone call, take a few minutes to ask about how things are going or to follow up on concerns expressed at the last meeting. Small group relationships go beyond the group meetings, and phone calls are good for ongoing relationship building.

Letters communicate detailed information. You might send a letter to announce the first group meeting, telling the new group's members what to expect and reminding them to bring Bibles. If a special event is coming up or if you want group members to be able to refer to a lot of information, a letter is a good choice.

---

[1] When group members experience crises always watch to see if they need more care than the group can provide. If so, help them find additional care from a pastor, a counselor, or another professional.

Postcards serve as quick reminders. You might use them to remind group members of an assignment or an upcoming event.

Greeting cards and personal notes are appropriate for birthdays, anniversaries, and graduations, as well as for expressions of sympathy and support.

Announcements—written or spoken—can.communicate information to the entire congregation. Use this form of communication when you are recruiting members or inviting the congregation to participate in something special your group is doing.

Who Should Communicate?

The group leader always has the final responsibility for communication between meetings, but you don't always need to be the one who makes contact. You may delegate some kinds of communication or encourage other group members to also make contact with one another.

Any group member who is able to write clearly can be given responsibility for letters, bulletin announcements, and reminder post cards. There are some people who make a personal ministry out of sending caring cards and notes to others.

In-person or telephone communication may be most effective when it comes from the small group leader (or apprentice) him- or herself. Communication works not only because of what a person says, but also because of who a person is. When you, the group leader, care enough to call and remind a member of the next meeting, the member is more likely to be there.

Reminder telephone calls can also be very effective coming from other group members. People you call may think you are calling, in part, because it is your responsibility to do so. When they receive a call from another group member, however, that feels like an expression of pure care.

Phone calls expressing care during difficult times

can come from any group member. In fact, the more people who make such calls the better.

Three Guidelines for Effective Communication

Effective communication with group members needs to be *redundant, clear,* and *personal.*

Communication must be *redundant* to be effective. Send a postcard in addition to the telephone call. Reinforce the written announcement with a spoken announcement. Since people are constantly bombarded with information, you need to make sure *your* information is part of the small percentage that is remembered, not the majority that is ignored or forgotten. Never expect one attempt at communicating to get the job done.

Make sure your communication is *clear.* Include details and never assume that people already know important facts. For example, if your group is going to meet in a different location, tell members the address and phone number of the location. Don't assume they already know even if they've been there once before, or that they will look it up in the church directory.

Person-to-person communication is by far the most effective. When possible, talk to group members in person or over the phone. Pay attention to their reactions to see if they have understood what you've said. Listen to their responses and clarify your communication if necessary. People often come to meetings, do assignments, or take leadership roles simply because someone who cares about them has personally asked them to do so.

CHAPTER 31

What to Do When You Must Miss a Meeting

Even a small group leader occasionally has to miss a meeting. This certainly shouldn't happen often, but it *will* happen at some time. When the leader must be absent, should the group just cancel the meeting? No. You need to arrange other leadership for the meeting.

When You Know You Will be Gone

When you know ahead of time that you'll be gone, you can delegate your normal group leader tasks. This gives group members a chance to practice *their* leadership skills.

The group's apprentice leader, if you have one, is the logical substitute. Filling in for you could be another way the apprentice gains leadership experience.

You could also arrange for several members of the group to share leadership tasks. One member might lead the prayer and worship, another the check-in discussion, and another the Biblical Equipping. If you divide the tasks among several group members, remember to choose one person who is responsible to oversee the whole meeting and make sure everything goes smoothly.

You may need to help the substitute leaders prepare. For example, go over the Scripture passage with the person leading Biblical Equipping. You may also want to call the leaders a few days ahead of time, so that you can answer any questions they have and make sure that they're prepared.

Planning for Unexpected Absences

Count on occasional unexpected absences. At

some point, something will come up at the last minute to keep you away from a group meeting: a car breakdown, a sudden attack of flu, or a sick baby-sitter. If you have a contingency plan already in place, the group can carry on without you.

Work with your apprentice, or with another group member, to develop a plan for leading a meeting if you can't be there. The plan should include:

- who will be substitute leader;
- a meeting agenda;
- a plan for the Biblical Equipping session; and
- leadership assignments for other group members.

A good contingency plan lets everyone know ahead of time what to do if the leader is absent. Designate one person who will lead the group in your absence. Everyone in the group needs to know who that person is, so they don't waste time trying to figure out who should lead. Let others know of any roles they might have, such as leading prayer or check-in time.

It's a good idea for the contingency leader to bring a folder to each group meeting containing an agenda and an already-prepared Biblical Equipping session—just in case. (This might also be kept on site if you have a place to store materials.) The agenda should be simple. The Biblical Equipping session need not relate to the Scriptures the group has been studying recently. It can cover general Christian beliefs from the Scriptures—something applicable and appropriate any time.

It's important that the contingency leader take responsibility assertively. When you call at the last minute to say you can't be at the meeting, or when it seems certain that you won't show up (and were unable to call), the contingency leader should remind the group of their contingency plan and begin the meeting right away.

CHAPTER 32

Welcoming Visitors to Your Small Group

Most groups welcome and encourage guests and new members. Open groups should expect people to visit. Group members who are excited about their groups naturally invite their friends to meetings. Again, when congregation members hear about small groups, they often decide to visit one to see for themselves what it's like. As small groups become better known, and as word gets out about how much members enjoy group meetings, you can expect your group to grow.

Some group members may be reluctant to welcome guests. They may like the group the way it is and feel uncomfortable when someone new comes to a meeting. Members may also feel less free to share deep feelings when there are guests at a group meeting. You need to help group members adjust to the changes that occur when guests come, and learn to welcome and honor newcomers, using Christ's love as an example.

How to Help Guests Feel Welcome

Treating Guests Hospitably

Hospitality is an important Christian trait. God welcomes us into his family, and group members imitate God's accepting love by welcoming others into the small group "family" God has given them.

Refer to Visitors as Guests

Make this standard practice in your group. Model it, and affirm group members when they remember to use this term. The way group members talk about guests will affect the way the guests are treated.

Treat Them Like Guests

When people visit, practice old-fashioned hospitality. Make sure your guests feel honored, welcome, and comfortable. For example, when guests arrive, a group member should take the person's coat, offer refreshments, and introduce him or her to other group members.

Help Guests Find a Place to Sit

Offer your guests a place to sit. Some guests may wonder if there's assigned seating, and your help will put them at ease. If a husband and wife visit, help them find a place to sit together.

Assign Guests a "Buddy"

Ask a group member to assist a guest during the session. Assistance might include sharing a Bible, answering questions, and explaining any group customs.

Include Guests in Group Activities

Small groups are participatory, so invite guests to participate in group activities as fully as they like. Guests should feel free to share about their lives, pray or request prayers, participate in the Biblical Equipping, and take part in the group's service activities.

Be careful, however, that you don't push guests to participate or share when they aren't comfortable doing so. Guests should be welcome to do everything everyone else does, or just to sit back and observe. Let them choose their own level of participation, and assure them that whatever they want to do is fine.

Should You Change Meeting Plans if Guests Are Present?

Occasionally groups wonder if they need to change their agenda when guests are present. This is not necessary. When guests are present you should go ahead and do what you planned. The only way a guest can understand what your group is like is to experience a regular meeting.

There is one time you might change your plans: if you had planned to settle a conflict or confront a difficult situation with a group member. For example, you may have a group member who has broken confidentiality or who is openly in conflict with another group member. In such a case, put off the challenging meeting content until another meeting, when you will be freer to deal with it and guests will not be made to feel uncomfortable.

What if the Guest Is Not a Christian?

If group members bring nonChristian guests, there's one rule to follow: Be yourselves, and allow the guests to do the same. There's no need to put all of your Christian activities and discussions on hold—it's unnecessary, and doesn't honor either the guest or the group. Instead, pray, read the Bible, and talk about God's love just as you normally would.

Of course, you shouldn't push your nonChristian guests to pray or take part in other activities which make them uncomfortable. Neither should you allow group members to argue with guests or put pressure on them. Your accepting, nonjudgmental care for them is a witness to God's accepting love for them.[1]

Trust God to work in the lives of your non-Christian guests. Your hospitality, your care, your discussion of Scripture and the ways God is leading you in your life all add up to a very good witness to Christ. Don't push anything more on guests. Eventually your guests may start asking questions, and then you can tell them more about Jesus.

Dealing with Discomfort

Even though you continue with the meeting you planned, having guests may inhibit other group members. This is understandable, but it is also something

---

[1] For a complete treatment of the benefits and effectiveness of process-oriented evangelism, see *Me, an Evangelist? Every Christian's Guide to Caring Evangelism* by William J. McKay (St. Louis: Stephen Ministries, 1992).

that group members can cope with when they are motivated by Christian love. Those who are uncomfortable sharing when guests are present can still share, although perhaps not as deeply they intended to. Group members may need to explain their comments more fully during Biblical Equipping when guests don't understand as much as everyone else about the Bible passage under discussion. Such situations give group members a chance to imitate Jesus, who gave up his rights for the sake of others—even to the point of dying on a cross (Philippians 2:6-8).

CHAPTER 33

Stay Focused on Jesus

Expect a lot of success as a small group leader. Your group will bond. Members will trust one another and share more deeply than they ever have before. You will see group members grow in their faith, trust Jesus more, and live as more fully devoted disciples. You will even see your small group reach out with Christ's love. You will have the privilege of seeing others' gratitude and sense of wonder as God works through your group to give them His gracious gift of love. All this will happen because the Holy Spirit is at work in and through you.

As you consider all the nuts and bolts choices in this book, and as you become caught up in the small group leader routine of caring, planning, communicating, praying, and deciding, remain focused on the *real* small group leader—Jesus.

Thank God for all he does in and through you, and for the small group he gives you to serve. Also remember Paul's words to the Philippians:

"If anyone else has reason to be confident in the flesh, I have more: circumcised on the eighth day, a member of the people of Israel, of the tribe of Benjamin, a Hebrew born of Hebrews; as to the law, a Pharisee; as to zeal, a persecutor of the church; as to righteousness under the law, blameless.

Yet whatever gains I had, these I have come to regard as loss because of Christ. More than that, I regard everything as loss because of the surpassing value of knowing Christ Jesus my Lord. For his sake I have suffered the loss of all things, and I regard

*them as rubbish, in order that I may gain
Christ and be found in him, not having a
righteousness of my own that comes from
the law, but one that comes through faith in
Christ, the righteousness from God based on
faith. I want to know Christ and the power of
his resurrection and the sharing of his suffer-
ings by becoming like him in his death, if
somehow I may attain the resurrection from
the dead"* (Philippians 3:4b-11).

In the midst of all your leading and deciding,
never lose sight of the fact that your group's success
and growth are unimportant when compared to the
surpassing value of knowing Jesus Christ your Lord.
The best way to help group members focus on Jesus
is to stay focused on him yourself.

Let your encouragement of group members'
prayer lives grow out of your own. Let your Biblical
Equipping leadership flow out of your own immer-
sion in God's Word. Commend your group, and yourself, into God's loving care. Then trust the Holy
Spirit to bless your work and the efforts and prayers
of group members, those who oversee your congregation's small group ministry, and the congregation. The
result will be a small group that lifts up Jesus Christ
and gives glory to his Father.

Accept this challenge with this promise: Regardless of how well you keep your focus on Jesus, he *will*
remain connected to you. He said, "My sheep hear my
voice. I know them, and they follow me. I give them
eternal life, and they will never perish. No one will
snatch them out of my hand. What my Father has
given me is greater than all else, and no one can
snatch it out of the Father's hand. The Father and I
are one" (John 10:27-30).

Because of Jesus' death and resurrection, you are
a child of God and you have eternal life. May that
promise strengthen you as you serve God and his people as a small group leader.

APPENDIX A

The ChristCare® Series

The ChristCare Series is a comprehensive system for leading and organizing small group ministry in the congregation.

Small group ministry is playing an increasingly important role in the mission of vital, missional congregations today. Small groups are a powerful tool to meet four important needs people have:

- spiritual growth;
- Christian community;
- mutual care;
- meaningful ministry.

Having one or two small groups in a congregation is relatively easy. To involve growing numbers of people in high quality small groups, however, is something that does not just happen. You need to plan and organize for it. You need key individuals trained to oversee and direct all the small groups in your congregation. Those key individuals train and supervise small group leaders, help people link up with groups, and manage the small group ministry for continuing growth.

This is where the ChristCare Series comes in. It provides a comprehensive system and complete training resources that are essential for quality, distinctively Christian small group ministry in the congregation.

Briefly, here are the steps a congregation follows to begin and maintain the ChristCare Series system of small group ministry:

1. Decide that your congregation wants to begin small group ministry, or improve and expand an already-existing small group ministry.

2. Explore the ChristCare Series by obtaining descriptive materials from Stephen Ministries, talking with others who are already using the ChristCare Series, and asking for God's guidance as you go through a decision-making process with the leaders of your congregation.

3. Enroll in the ChristCare Series and receive a *Vision Building Kit* from Stephen Ministries, which you will use to build a solid foundation for small group ministry.

4. Recruit and select a team of at least two or more ChristCare Equippers. Equippers are pastors and lay leaders who are trained at a seven-day Equipper's Training Course (ETC) to direct every aspect of their congregation's ChristCare Group Ministry.

5. Send Equippers to the seven-day Equipper's Training Course. Following are a few of the topics covered at each ETC:

   - Building an Effective Team of ChristCare Equippers

   - The Theology and Practice of Christian Community

   - How to Build Membership in ChristCare Groups and Grow Your ChristCare Group Ministry

   - The Care and Nurture of Apprentice ChristCare Group Leaders

   - Supplying Resources for ChristCare Group Activities

   - How to Supervise ChristCare Group Leaders: **S**upport, **E**ncouragement, and **A**ccountability (SEA) Groups

   - Successful Models for ChristCare Group Ministry: How ChristCare Groups Support Your Congregation's Mission

   - And more . . .

6. Support your trained ChristCare Equippers as they return to your congregation and . . .

- build a solid foundation for ChristCare Group Ministry;
- recruit and select ChristCare Group Leaders;
- train ChristCare Group Leaders using the *ChristCare Group Leader Training Manual*;
- commission ChristCare Group Leaders;
- direct ChristCare Group Leaders as they begin small groups and build membership in groups;
- conduct ongoing **S**upport, **E**ncouragement, and **A**ccountability (SEA) Groups for ChristCare Group Leaders;
- recognize and affirm ChristCare Equippers and ChristCare Group Leaders;
- coordinate ChristCare Group Ministry with other ministries in your congregation; and
- continue this series of activities as the congregation's small group ministry grows and reaches more and more people—inside and outside the congregation.

7. Send additional members to an Equipper's Training Course in future years to ensure the ongoing effectiveness of ChristCare Group Ministry.

Following are some of the topics the ChristCare Series provides to ChristCare Equippers who, in turn, train ChristCare Group Leaders for effective small group leadership in the congregation:

- Building Community in Your Small Group
- Being a Process-Oriented Leader
- How to Effectively Participate in a SEA Group
- The Nuts and Bolts of Leading a Small Group
- Listening Skills for Small Group Leaders
- Confidentiality in Small Groups
- How to Use the Bible as an Equipping Tool
- Assertiveness Skills for Small Group Leaders
- Evangelism in and through Small Groups

- Birthing New Small Groups

- And more . . .

The ChristCare Series provides comprehensive organization and thorough training that result in high quality, distinctively Christian, mission-minded small groups in the congregation.

The ChristCare Series works very effectively in combination with the Stephen Series system of one-to-one lay caring ministry described in Appendix B. Among many other benefits, the Stephen Series provides an important "safety valve" for small groups that have a member who needs more care than the group can appropriately provide. A Stephen Series congregation has trained and supervised lay caregivers ready to provide individual, ongoing care for these people, who can continue meeting with their group as they receive the personalized care they need. Rather than spending large amounts of time on one individual, the small group then can care for all its members and more effectively carry out its mission. Also, Stephen Ministers (trained lay caregivers) may invite care receivers to consider ChristCare Groups as an excellent way to further their spiritual growth in a caring Christian community.

When you contact Stephen Ministries for information about the ChristCare Series, the Stephen Series, or both, also request a copy of the booklet, *How the Stephen Series and the ChristCare Series Can Work Together in the Same Congregation*. It describes how both ministry systems meet distinct, important, and complementary ministry needs. Congregations with both the ChristCare Series and the Stephen Series are able to equip many more people for service and leadership that expands dramatically the congregation's capacity for spiritual nurture, mission outreach, and caring ministry.

For a packet of descriptive materials about the ChristCare Series, contact *Stephen Ministries, 8016 Dale, St. Louis, Missouri 63117-1449, or call 314/645-5511, FAX 314/645-9133.*

APPENDIX B

The Stephen Series®

*The Stephen Series is a complete system
for training and organizing
lay persons for caring ministry in and
around their congregations.*

The Stephen Series works! Since the beginning of the Stephen Series in 1975, thousands of congregations representing over 75 denominations have enrolled in the Stephen Series. They have successfully established one-to-one lay caring ministry systems as part of their ongoing outreach to hurting and suffering people.

How does it work? Briefly, these are the steps a congregation follows to establish a caring ministry that grows with people as it helps people grow:

1. Assess your congregation's need for caring ministry. Are there needs for care that are not being met at the present time?

2. Investigate the Stephen Series as a possible system to meet these needs. Stephen Ministries has informational packets available to help with this.

3. Enroll in the Stephen Series and receive from Stephen Ministries preliminary materials to begin preparing the congregation for this ministry.

4. Carefully select one or more representatives to attend a seven-day Leader's Training Course (LTC) to become Stephen Leaders. Following are some of the areas covered at each LTC to train members to lead this ministry in their congregations:

   • Helping Your Congregation Understand and Believe in the Value of Stephen Ministry

- Finding the Right People for the Right Ministry: How to Recruit and Select Stephen Ministers
- When to Refer a Care Receiver for Professional Help
- How to Find and Prepare Care Receivers for Your Stephen Ministers
- How to Maintain High Quality Caring through Small Group Peer Supervision
- Methods and Resources for Continuing Education
- How Pastors and Lay Leaders Can Tangibilify Their Support for Stephen Ministry
- And more . . .

5. Encourage trained Stephen Leaders who return to your congregation and . . .
   - recruit and select individuals to train as Stephen Ministers;
   - continue to build support for Stephen Ministry in the congregation;
   - provide a minimum of 50 hours of training for Stephen Ministers;
   - commission those trained as Stephen Ministers;
   - link Stephen Ministers with the persons to whom they will minister;
   - implement the Stephen Series model of small group peer supervision and continuing education for the Stephen Ministers, and;
   - continue the cycle of recruiting, training, referring, and supervising Stephen Ministers to meet the caring needs of the congregation.

6. Ensure the ongoing effectiveness of Stephen Ministry in your congregation by sending additional members to Leader's Training Courses in future years.

Following are some of the modules the Stephen Series provides to Stephen Leaders to train Stephen Ministers in the congregation:

- Feelings: Yours, Mine, and Ours
- The Art of Listening
- Ministering to Those Experiencing Divorce
- How to Make a First Caring Visit
- Confidentiality
- Using Community Resources
- Crisis Theory and Practice: Danger vs. Opportunity
- Assertiveness: Relating Gently and Firmly
- Ministering to Those Experiencing Grief
- Supervision: A Key to Quality Christian Care
- And more . . .

Comprehensive organization and thorough training result in high quality, distinctively Christian, lay caring ministry in the congregation.

The Stephen Series works very effectively in combination with the ChristCare Series system of small group ministry described in Appendix A. Among many other benefits, the Stephen Series provides an important "safety valve" for small groups that have a member who needs more care than the group can appropriately provide. A Stephen Series congregation has trained and supervised lay caregivers ready to provide individual, ongoing care for these people, who can continue meeting with their group as they receive the personalized care they need. Rather than spending large amounts of time on one individual, the small group then can care for all its members and more effectively carry out its mission. Also, Stephen Ministers (trained lay caregivers) may invite care receivers to consider ChristCare Groups as an excellent way to further their spiritual growth in a caring Christian community.

When you contact Stephen Ministries for information about the Stephen Series, the ChristCare Series, or both, also request a copy of the booklet, *How the Stephen Series and the ChristCare Series*

Can Work Together in the Same Congregation. It describes how both ministry systems meet distinct, important, and complementary ministry needs. Congregations with both the Stephen Series and the ChristCare Series are able to equip many more people for service and leadership that expands dramatically the congregation's capacity for spiritual nurture, mission outreach, and caring ministry.

For a packet of descriptive materials about the Stephen Series contact *Stephen Ministries, 8016 Dale, St. Louis, Missouri 63117-1449, or call 314/645-5511, FAX 314/645-9133.*

Index